The AI-Augmented Salesperson

A Practical Guide to Selling Smarter

Sidney Anderson, PhD

AR Consultancy LLC

An AR Consultancy LLC Book

The AI-Augmented Salesperson: A Practical Guide to Selling Smarter

© 2026 by Sidney Anderson

All rights reserved.

Cover design by Muzammil Yaqoob

ISBN 978-1-971262-34-5 (hardcover) | ISBN 978-1-971262-32-1 (paperback) | ISBN 978-1-971262-33-8 (ebook) | LCCN 2026900357

This book offers educational content and perspectives on artificial intelligence applications in sales, technology adoption, and professional development based on research, observation, and conceptual frameworks. The author and publisher provide this material for informational purposes only. Nothing in this publication constitutes legal advice, financial guidance, technology consulting, employment counseling, or professional consulting for specific business situations. The author and publisher have endeavored to ensure quality and accuracy in this work. However, no guarantees are made regarding the completeness, reliability, or applicability of the content. AI technologies evolve rapidly, and specific tools, features, and capabilities discussed may change after publication. Readers must evaluate whether the concepts and approaches discussed are appropriate for their individual professional circumstances. No warranty of suitability for any specific purpose is expressed or implied. Should you require guidance on legal, financial, regulatory, technology implementation, data privacy, employment, or compliance matters, consult qualified professionals in those respective fields. The frameworks and strategies in this book are educational tools, not professional services. This publication does not replace expert legal, financial, technical, or consulting advice tailored to your specific situation. Results from applying sales techniques and AI tools vary based on individual circumstances, market conditions, technology platforms, and numerous other factors beyond the author's control.

This work is protected by copyright law. No part of this publication may be copied, reproduced, scanned, distributed, or transmitted in any medium or format without express written consent from the author and publisher.

For author inquiries: standersonbooks@gmail.com

Contents

Introduction	VII
1. The New Sales Landscape	1
2. AI Fundamentals for Sales Professionals	13
3. Finding the Right Prospects	29
4. Understanding Your Customer	43
5. Personalization at Scale	58
6. The Efficiency Edge	73
7. What AI Can't Do	87
8. Earning Trust in an Automated World	100
9. Building Your AI-Ready Career	115
10. AI in Complex Negotiations	130
11. Leading AI-Augmented Sales Teams	144
12. Building Your AI Sales Stack	160
13. Measuring AI Impact	175
14. Ethics and Responsibility in AI-Powered Sales	189
15. The Road Ahead	208

16. Self-Assessment Guide: Your AI-Augmented Sales Readiness   228

Introduction

Maria stared at her laptop screen at 6:47 AM, coffee growing cold beside her. Her territory had just expanded by forty percent, but her quota had grown even faster. The math didn't work. She couldn't possibly research, contact, and nurture that many prospects while maintaining the relationships that made her a top performer. Something had to give.

Three months later, Maria sat in the same chair, but the math had changed. Her AI assistant had flagged twelve accounts showing sudden spikes in relevant website activity. It had drafted personalized outreach for each, drawing on news about their recent funding rounds and executive changes. It had summarized her last conversations with existing clients and reminded her that one buyer's contract renewal was approaching. By 7:30 AM, she had accomplished what previously took until noon. By quarter's end, she had exceeded her expanded quota by eighteen percent.

Maria isn't a fictional character. She's a composite of dozens of sales professionals I've interviewed over the past year. Her story captures something important: AI didn't replace what made her successful. It removed the friction that was holding her back.

Why This Book Exists

The conversation about AI in sales has become polarized. On one side, breathless predictions suggest that AI will automate salespeople out of existence within a decade. On the other, skeptics dismiss AI as over-hyped technology that can't handle the nuance of human relationships. Both camps are wrong. The reality is more interesting and more useful. AI and sales aren't competing forces. They're complementary capabilities that, when combined thoughtfully, produce results neither can achieve alone. This book explores that combination. It's written for sales professionals who want practical guidance rather than speculation, and who recognize that understanding AI has become a career necessity rather than an optional curiosity. I won't promise that reading this book will transform you overnight or guarantee your success. What I will promise is an honest examination of what AI can do for your sales practice, what it can't do, and how to navigate the difference.

The Indispensable Technology

AI has moved from research labs to sales floors because it solves problems that have plagued the profession for decades.

The information problem. Sales has always been information-intensive work. Who should I call? What do they care about? When are they ready to buy? What happened in our last conversation? Salespeople have historically spent enormous energy gathering, organizing, and recalling information. AI processes information at a scale and speed that humans simply can't match. It identifies patterns across thousands of data points, surfaces relevant insights at the moment of need, and maintains perfect memory of every interaction.

The time problem. Studies consistently show that salespeople spend less than a third of their time actually selling. The rest disappears into administrative work, data entry, meeting preparation, and research. AI automates much of this burden. It drafts emails, summarizes calls, updates CRM records, and handles scheduling. Every hour reclaimed is an hour available for the human work that closes deals.

The personalization problem. Buyers expect relevance. They don't want generic pitches or mass-produced content. They want salespeople who understand their specific situation and can address their particular needs. But genuine personalization takes time, and time is finite. AI enables personalization at scale by analyzing customer data, tailoring messaging, and helping salespeople show up prepared for every conversation.

The prediction problem. Which deals will close? Which prospects are worth pursuing? Where should I focus my limited attention? Sales has always involved educated guessing. AI improves those guesses by analyzing historical patterns and identifying signals that correlate with success. It doesn't make prediction perfect, but it makes it meaningfully better.

These aren't marginal improvements. Organizations that implement AI effectively report significant gains in productivity, conversion rates, and revenue per salesperson. The technology has crossed the threshold from interesting to indispensable.

The Irreplaceable Function

While AI has grown in importance, the fundamental value of sales hasn't diminished. If anything, it has increased. Sales is how organizations create customers. Marketing can generate awareness and interest. Product development can build solutions. Operations can deliver value. But sales converts potential into revenue. It's the function that turns a company's capabilities into cash flow, and cash flow is what keeps organizations alive.

This isn't merely a financial observation. Sales serves as the connective tissue between what a company offers and what customers actually need. Good salespeople don't just push products. They translate. They listen to customer problems and connect them to solutions. They gather market intelligence and bring it back to product teams. They build relationships that create long-term value rather than one-time transactions. Companies that underinvest in sales capability pay the price. They build products that don't find markets. They lose customers to competitors who engage more effectively. They struggle to grow even when their offerings are superior. The graveyard of failed businesses is filled with organizations that had good technology, good ideas, or good intentions but couldn't sell.

The rise of AI doesn't change this equation. Complex purchases still require human trust. Strategic partnerships still depend on relationship depth. High-value customers still expect to work with people who understand them. AI handles information and efficiency. Humans handle connection and judgment. Both are necessary.

The Synergy

Here's what makes the current moment so interesting for sales professionals: AI and human capability don't just coexist. They amplify each other. Consider what happens when a skilled salesperson gains access to AI tools. Their existing strengths become more powerful. Strong relationship builders can maintain more relationships because AI handles the administrative load. Skilled negotiators can prepare more thoroughly because AI surfaces relevant information. Persuasive communicators can reach more prospects because AI helps them personalize at scale.

The reverse is also true. AI becomes more valuable in the hands of skilled salespeople. The insights AI generates are only useful if someone knows how to act on them. The time AI saves only matters if it's reinvested in high-value activities. The personalization AI enables only works if a human ensures it feels genuine rather than mechanical. This synergy creates an opportunity for sales professionals willing to embrace it. Those who learn to work effectively with AI will outperform those who don't. Not because AI does their job for them, but because AI removes the obstacles that prevent them from doing their job well.

What Lies Ahead

This book is organized around a simple progression. We'll start with the foundational understanding you need to evaluate AI tools and opportunities. We'll move through specific applications across the sales process, from prospecting to closing. We'll address the human elements that AI can't replicate and the trust considerations that arise when AI enters customer relationships. We'll finish with career guidance and a look at where the technology is heading. Throughout, the focus is practical. I'm less interested in what AI might theoretically accomplish and more interested in what it can do for you today. Each chapter includes frameworks you can apply, questions you should ask, and pitfalls you should avoid.

I also want to be clear about what this book isn't. It's not a product guide that will become obsolete when the next tool launches. It's not a technical manual that requires engineering knowledge. It's not a collection of success stories designed to make AI seem magical. The goal is durable understanding that helps you navigate whatever specific tools and situations you encounter. Sales has always rewarded those who adapt. The Rolodex gave way to the database. Cold calling gave way to social selling. Each transition created winners and losers based on who embraced change and who resisted it. AI represents the next transition. The professionals who thrive won't be those who fear AI or those who worship it. They'll be those who understand it clearly and use it wisely. That understanding starts here.

Chapter One

The New Sales Landscape

A Profession Built on Adaptation

Sales is one of the oldest professions, and one of the most frequently transformed. Every generation of salespeople has faced a technology shift that rewrote the rules of their work. The filing cabinet gave way to the Rolodex. The Rolodex gave way to contact management software. Contact management software gave way to customer relationship management platforms. Each transition felt disruptive at the time. Each created temporary winners and losers. And each ultimately became so embedded in standard practice that younger salespeople can't imagine working without it.

Consider the CRM transition. When Salesforce launched its cloud-based platform, many sales veterans resisted. They had systems that worked. They knew where their contacts lived, what they had discussed, and when to follow up. Why change? But the salespeople who adopted CRM technology gained advantages their peers couldn't match: centralized data, automated reminders, pipeline visibility, and collaboration across teams. Within a decade, CRM adoption wasn't optional. It was table stakes.

AI represents the next shift in this long history. Like previous transitions, it's generating resistance, confusion, and uneven adoption. Like previous transitions, it will ultimately separate those who adapt from those who don't. The question isn't whether AI will reshape sales. It already has. The question is whether you'll be positioned on the right side of that change.

What Actually Changed

AI isn't new. Researchers have worked on machine learning and natural language processing for decades. So why does AI matter for sales now, when it didn't five years ago? Three developments converged to make this moment different.

Processing power became cheap. The algorithms behind modern AI require enormous computational resources. Training a large language model can require thousands of specialized processors running for weeks. This capacity didn't exist at accessible price points until recently. Cloud computing changed the economics, allowing a salesperson to access AI capabilities that would have required a supercomputer a generation ago, all through a monthly subscription. This democratization leveled the playing field. Early CRM systems cost hundreds of thousands and required dedicated IT teams, leaving small organizations behind. AI followed a different path. Cloud computing distributes costs across millions of users, giving a solo consultant access to the same capability as a Fortune 500 salesperson. Adoption isn't gated by budget. It's gated by willingness to learn.

At the same time, data became abundant. AI learns from data, and the more relevant data available, the more capable the AI becomes. The explosion of digital interaction has created unprecedented data resources. Every email, every call recording, every website visit, every CRM entry becomes potential training material. Sales organizations now generate enough data to feed AI systems that can identify patterns humans would never detect. A decade ago, most customer interactions happened offline and left no trace. Today, the digital footprint of a typical sales relationship includes thousands of data points that AI can analyze for signals about intent, satisfaction, and likelihood to buy.

Finally, interfaces became usable. Early AI required technical expertise to operate. You needed to write code, understand model architectures, and interpret raw outputs. Modern AI tools hide this complexity behind intuitive interfaces. A salesperson can now ask a question in plain language and receive a useful answer without understanding anything about the underlying technology. This shift mirrors what happened with computers generally. The first business computers required specialized operators. Then came command-line interfaces that demanded technical knowledge. Then graphical interfaces that anyone could navigate. AI has compressed this evolution into just a few years, moving from research tool to everyday assistant.

These three factors created a tipping point. AI moved from research curiosity to practical tool. For sales professionals, this shift happened quickly. Tools that seemed experimental two years ago are now standard features in major sales platforms.

The Fear and the Reality

When new technology threatens to change how work gets done, fear is a natural response. Sales professionals watching AI development have legitimate questions. Will AI take my job? Will it commoditize my skills? Will I become obsolete if I don't become a technologist? These fears deserve direct answers.

The concern about job loss is understandable, but the reality is nuanced. Some roles will disappear. Transactional sales positions that involve little more than order-taking and information delivery are vulnerable. If a customer can get the same information from a chatbot, they will. But complex sales, relationship sales, enterprise sales, and consultative sales require capabilities AI doesn't possess. These roles won't disappear. They'll evolve. The pattern mirrors what happened with ATMs and bank tellers. When ATMs arrived, analysts predicted the end of the teller role. Instead, the number of bank branches increased because ATMs reduced the cost of operating each branch. Teller jobs shifted from transaction processing to relationship building and complex service. AI will likely produce a similar dynamic in sales: fewer people doing routine tasks, more people doing high-value work.

The fear that AI will commoditize sales skills actually gets the dynamic backwards. The opposite is more likely. AI raises the baseline of what every salesperson can accomplish. When everyone has access to AI-powered research, prospecting, and personalization, the differentiator becomes what you do with those capabilities. Judgment, creativity, and relationship skills become more valuable, not less, because the routine work that used to consume time no longer provides competitive separation.

As for whether you need to become a technologist, the answer is no. You need to become an effective user of technology, which is different. You don't need to understand how your CRM's database architecture works to use it well. You don't need to understand neural network mathematics to use AI well. You need enough conceptual understanding to evaluate tools, ask good questions, and recognize both capabilities and limitations. That's the level this book aims to provide.

Where AI Creates Advantage

Understanding where AI helps requires understanding what AI does well. Four capabilities matter most for sales, and they work together to transform what individual salespeople can accomplish. The first is pattern recognition at scale. Humans excel at recognizing patterns in small data sets. We can look at ten deals and notice that three had something in common. AI recognizes patterns across thousands or millions of data points, identifying correlations that no human could detect. Which combination of firmographic and behavioral signals predicts purchase intent? AI can answer that question with statistical rigor. A regional software company analyzed three years of closed deals and discovered that prospects who visited their pricing page more than twice, downloaded a specific technical whitepaper, and had recently posted job listings for relevant roles converted at four times the average rate. No salesperson would have identified that pattern manually. With AI, the pattern became a prospecting filter that transformed their pipeline quality.

The second capability is speed of information processing. Sales involves enormous information flows. Calls generate transcripts. Emails pile up. News breaks about prospects and competitors. Market conditions shift. No human can process all relevant information in real time. AI can. It summarizes calls while you're still on them. It monitors news about your accounts. It tracks competitor movements. It surfaces what matters and filters what doesn't.

Third, AI delivers consistency without fatigue. Humans get tired, distracted, and inconsistent. The twentieth call of the day rarely matches the energy of the first. AI doesn't fatigue. It applies the same criteria to the thousandth lead score that it applied to the first. It sends follow-up reminders regardless of how busy the week becomes. It catches details that slip past exhausted human attention.

Fourth, AI enables personalization without proportional effort. Crafting a genuinely personalized message takes time. Multiply that time by hundreds of prospects, and personalization becomes impossible to sustain. AI changes the math. It can tailor content to individual recipients based on their industry, role, company situation, and previous interactions. The salesperson reviews and refines rather than creating from scratch.

Where AI Falls Short

Knowing what AI can't do matters as much as knowing what it can. Overestimating AI capabilities leads to poor decisions about where to invest human attention. The most significant limitation is that AI doesn't build trust. Customers buy from people they trust. Trust develops through consistent behavior over time, through demonstrated understanding of customer needs, through reliability when things go wrong. AI can support trust-building by ensuring salespeople show up prepared and follow through on commitments. But the trust itself forms between humans. No algorithm substitutes for genuine human connection in high-stakes purchasing decisions.

Closely related is that AI doesn't navigate ambiguity well. Real sales conversations involve subtext, emotion, unstated objections, and organizational politics. A customer says "we're not ready to move forward" but means "I can't get my boss on board." A procurement officer raises price objections when the real issue is risk aversion. AI struggles with this kind of interpretation. It processes explicit content effectively but misses the layers of meaning that experienced salespeople read instinctively.

AI also doesn't exercise judgment in the way sales situations demand. When should you push and when should you step back? When does persistence become annoyance? When should you walk away from a deal that isn't right for the customer? These decisions require wisdom that comes from experience, values, and contextual understanding. AI can provide information to inform judgment. It can't replace it.

Finally, AI doesn't create genuine relationships. Some customers become long-term partners, sources of referrals, and professional friends. These relationships develop through shared experiences, mutual respect, and authentic human interaction. AI can help you maintain relationships by tracking details and prompting outreach. But the relationship itself exists between people.

The Complementary Model

The most useful way to think about AI in sales isn't replacement or competition. It's complementarity. AI and human salespeople have different strengths. When combined thoughtfully, they produce outcomes neither achieves alone. Consider a practical example. David sells enterprise software to manufacturing companies. Before AI tools, his process looked like this: spend Monday morning researching target accounts, dedicate Tuesday to drafting personalized outreach, allocate Wednesday through Friday to calls and meetings, then repeat. Research and preparation consumed forty percent of his selling time.

With AI tools, David's process changed. He starts each morning reviewing AI-generated briefings on his target accounts. The system has monitored news, tracked website activity, analyzed financial filings, and flagged relevant changes. Draft outreach messages wait for his review, personalized based on each prospect's situation. He edits rather than creates, approves rather than drafts. His research and preparation time dropped to fifteen percent of his week. The other twenty-five percent shifted to customer conversations.

David didn't become less important to the sales process. He became more focused on the parts where he adds unique value. AI handles information gathering and initial content creation. David handles relationship building, complex questioning, and judgment about how to position solutions. Each does what it does best. This complementary model defines the future of sales work. The salespeople who thrive won't be those who resist AI or those who expect AI to do their jobs. They'll be those who develop clear understanding of where the boundary lies and who optimize their effort on the human side of that boundary.

The Adoption Curve

Not every sales organization has embraced AI, and not every salesperson has developed relevant skills. This uneven adoption creates opportunity for those who move early. Early adopters are already seeing measurable results. Research across industries shows consistent patterns: sales teams using AI tools effectively report higher productivity, better conversion rates, and increased revenue per salesperson. The gains aren't marginal. Organizations report double-digit percentage improvements across key metrics.

Meanwhile, late adopters face growing competitive disadvantage. When your competitor's salespeople can personalize at scale while you're still crafting individual emails manually, you lose. When their team identifies high-intent prospects automatically while yours relies on gut instinct, you lose. When they spend time on customer conversations while you spend time on data entry, you lose. The window of advantage from early adoption narrows as adoption spreads. Salespeople who develop AI skills now position themselves ahead of peers who will eventually catch up. They build expertise while others are still learning basics. They establish track records while others are still experimenting.

This isn't speculation. It's the same pattern that played out with CRM adoption, social selling, and every previous technology transition. Early movers gain advantage. Fast followers catch up. Laggards struggle. The only question is which group you'll join.

What This Means for Your Career

Career implications flow directly from the landscape described above, and they're arriving faster than many professionals expect. AI competency is becoming a baseline expectation. Just as no serious sales candidate today can claim ignorance of CRM systems, no serious sales candidate in the near future will be able to claim ignorance of AI tools. Hiring managers will expect familiarity. Interview questions will probe for experience. Job descriptions will list AI-related requirements. At the same time, competitive differentiation is shifting to human skills. When AI handles research, preparation, and routine communication, the ability to build trust, navigate ambiguity, exercise judgment, and create relationships becomes the basis for standing out. These skills have always mattered. They'll matter more.

Adaptability is becoming essential as well. AI capabilities are evolving quickly. The tools available today will be superseded by more powerful tools tomorrow. Salespeople who learn to evaluate, adopt, and master new tools continuously will outperform those who learn one system and stop. The skill isn't mastery of any particular tool. It's the meta-skill of rapid technology adoption. And as AI handles more tactical execution, strategic thinking grows in value. AI excels at optimization within defined parameters. Humans excel at questioning whether the parameters are right. Salespeople who can step back, see patterns, and make decisions about where to focus will be more valuable than those who simply execute.

These career implications aren't distant futures. They're present realities accelerating quickly. The salespeople who recognize this and act accordingly will build careers that grow stronger as AI capabilities expand. Those who dismiss or ignore AI will find their options narrowing.

The Path Forward

Embracing AI in sales doesn't require abandoning what makes salespeople effective. It requires integrating new capabilities with existing strengths. The journey starts with understanding. You need enough knowledge of AI fundamentals to evaluate tools, recognize limitations, and make informed decisions. You don't need technical depth. You need conceptual clarity. From understanding comes application. Each stage of the sales process offers opportunities for AI integration. Prospecting, research, outreach, qualification, presentation, negotiation, and relationship management all have AI applications worth exploring. Some will transform your work. Others won't fit your situation.

Application leads to optimization. As you gain experience with AI tools, you'll develop intuitions about where they help and where they hinder. You'll learn when to trust AI recommendations and when to override them. You'll find your own balance between automation and human judgment. Throughout this progression, the goal isn't to become dependent on AI or to resist it. The goal is to develop a productive working relationship that amplifies your strengths and compensates for your limitations. That relationship will evolve as AI capabilities change. The salespeople who build it thoughtfully will find themselves better positioned with each evolution.

The following chapters provide the knowledge and frameworks you need to navigate this path. We'll start with the fundamentals you need to understand AI capabilities and evaluate the tools that promise to deliver them.

Chapter Two

AI Fundamentals for Sales Professionals

Why Fundamentals Matter

You don't need to become a data scientist to use AI effectively in sales. But you do need enough understanding to separate genuine capability from marketing hype. Vendors will make claims. Some will be accurate. Many won't be. Without foundational knowledge, you can't tell the difference.

Consider the salesperson evaluating two prospecting tools. Both promise "AI-powered lead scoring." One uses sophisticated machine learning trained on millions of successful sales outcomes. The other applies basic rules that marketing labeled as AI for competitive positioning. These tools will produce dramatically different results, but their marketing materials look nearly identical. The salesperson who understands AI fundamentals can ask the right questions and make an informed choice. The salesperson who doesn't will guess.

This chapter provides the conceptual foundation you need. We'll cover the core technologies behind AI sales tools, explain how they work in plain language, and connect each technology to specific sales applications. The goal isn't technical mastery. It's working fluency that helps you evaluate tools, understand their limitations, and apply them effectively.

Machine Learning: Finding Patterns in Data

Machine learning is the foundation of most AI applications in sales. The core idea is straightforward: instead of programming a computer with explicit rules, you feed it data and let it discover patterns on its own. Traditional software follows instructions. If a customer's annual revenue exceeds $10 million and they're in the technology sector and they've visited the pricing page, flag them as high priority. A programmer writes these rules based on assumptions about what matters. The software executes exactly what it's told.

Machine learning works differently. You provide the system with historical data about past deals, including which ones closed and which ones didn't. The system analyzes this data, looking for patterns that distinguish winners from losers. Maybe it discovers that pricing page visits matter, but only when combined with specific job titles and certain email engagement patterns. Maybe it finds correlations no human would have guessed. The machine learns the rules from the data rather than receiving them from a programmer. This distinction has practical implications for sales. Rule-based systems can only capture what their designers already know. Machine learning systems can discover what nobody knew. A sales organization might believe that company size predicts deal success, but machine learning analysis reveals that growth rate matters more. That insight changes prospecting strategy.

Machine learning comes in several varieties. Supervised learning trains on labeled examples. You show the system thousands of leads marked as "converted" or "didn't convert," and it learns to predict which category new leads will fall into. Unsupervised learning finds structure in unlabeled data. You feed it customer information without predetermined categories, and it identifies natural groupings you might use for segmentation. Reinforcement learning improves through trial and error. A system that optimizes email send times might test different approaches, measure results, and gradually learn what works best for different customer types. For sales applications, supervised learning drives most of the tools you'll encounter. Lead scoring, deal prediction, churn forecasting, and recommendation engines typically rely on supervised learning trained on historical outcomes.

Neural Networks: Learning Complex Relationships

Some patterns are too complex for traditional machine learning to capture. Neural networks handle this complexity by processing information through layers of interconnected nodes, loosely inspired by how biological neurons connect in the brain. Think of a neural network as a series of filters. Raw data enters the first layer. That layer identifies basic features and passes them to the next layer. The next layer combines basic features into more complex patterns. Each subsequent layer builds higher-level understanding from lower-level inputs.

By the final layer, the network can recognize sophisticated patterns that would be impossible to specify explicitly.

Image recognition illustrates this clearly. Early layers detect edges and shapes. Middle layers combine edges into features like eyes, noses, and mouths. Later layers assemble features into face recognition. No programmer wrote rules for identifying faces. The network learned by processing millions of labeled images.

In sales contexts, neural networks power applications that require understanding complex, unstructured information. Conversation intelligence platforms use neural networks to analyze call recordings, identifying not just words but tone, sentiment, and conversational dynamics. Email analysis tools use them to understand message content beyond simple keyword matching. Recommendation engines use them to identify subtle patterns in customer behavior that predict product interest.

The power of neural networks comes with a tradeoff. They're often "black boxes" that produce useful outputs without explaining their reasoning. A neural network might accurately predict which deals will close, but it can't articulate why in terms humans easily understand. This opacity creates challenges for salespeople who want to learn from AI insights rather than just follow them. We'll address strategies for managing this limitation later in the chapter.

Natural Language Processing: Understanding Human Communication

Natural language processing, or NLP, enables machines to work with human language. This matters enormously for sales because sales runs on language. Emails, calls, presentations, proposals, and contracts are all language artifacts. AI that can read, understand, and generate language transforms what's possible. NLP has evolved dramatically in recent years. Early systems relied on rigid rules and pattern matching. They could identify keywords and follow scripts but couldn't handle the flexibility and ambiguity of real human communication. Modern NLP uses neural networks trained on vast amounts of text, enabling genuine understanding of meaning, context, and nuance. The capabilities break into several categories relevant to sales.

Text analysis extracts information and meaning from written content. An NLP system can read a prospect's annual report, press releases, and social media posts, then summarize key themes, identify strategic priorities, and flag potential pain points. A salesperson would need hours to accomplish the same analysis. NLP does it in seconds.

Sentiment analysis determines emotional tone. Is this customer email frustrated or satisfied? Is this product review positive or negative? Is this social media mention a threat or an opportunity? Sentiment analysis processes language to answer these questions at scale, enabling salespeople to prioritize responses and identify at-risk accounts before problems escalate.

Conversation intelligence analyzes sales calls and meetings. Modern platforms transcribe conversations in real time, identify key moments like objections and commitments, track talk-time ratios between rep and customer, and flag coaching opportunities. A sales manager reviewing calls manually might sample a few per week. Conversation intelligence analyzes every call.

Language generation produces human-like text. This capability powers email drafting, proposal generation, and content personalization. You provide context and parameters. The AI generates a draft that sounds natural and addresses the specific situation. The salesperson reviews, edits, and sends rather than writing from scratch.

These NLP capabilities compound when combined. An AI assistant might analyze a prospect's recent communications, identify that they're expressing frustration with their current vendor, draft a personalized outreach email that addresses their likely pain points, and suggest optimal send timing based on their historical response patterns. Each step involves different NLP capabilities working together.

Predictive Analytics: Forecasting What Comes Next

Predictive analytics uses historical data to forecast future outcomes. For sales, this means answering questions that have always required guesswork: Which leads will convert? Which deals will close? Which customers will churn? When will prospects be ready to buy? The underlying approach combines statistics with machine learning. Historical data provides the foundation. The system identifies which factors correlate with outcomes of interest. It builds a model that weights these factors and produces predictions for new cases.

Consider lead scoring. A predictive lead scoring system analyzes thousands of historical leads, examining which ones converted and which ones didn't. It identifies patterns: certain industries convert at higher rates, specific behavioral signals indicate buying readiness, particular combinations of firmographic data predict good fit. When a new lead enters the system, it applies these learned patterns to generate a score predicting conversion likelihood. The quality of predictions depends heavily on data quality and quantity. Systems trained on small data sets produce unreliable predictions. Systems trained on biased data reproduce those biases. Systems trained on outdated data miss changes in buying patterns. Understanding these dependencies helps you evaluate predictive tools and interpret their outputs appropriately.

Predictive analytics also surfaces leading indicators that help salespeople intervene before outcomes are determined. A churn prediction model might identify that customers who reduce login frequency and submit more support tickets are likely to cancel. This gives account managers the opportunity to reach out proactively rather than reacting after the customer has already decided to leave. For sales forecasting specifically, predictive models analyze pipeline data to estimate likely bookings. They consider deal stages, historical progression rates, salesperson track records, seasonal patterns, and dozens of other factors. These forecasts typically outperform human intuition, particularly for aggregate predictions across large pipelines.

Large Language Models: The Current Frontier

Large language models represent the most visible recent advance in AI. These systems train on enormous text datasets, learning patterns of human language that enable remarkable capabilities in understanding and generation. The scale of these models matters. Earlier NLP systems trained on millions of words. Large language models train on hundreds of billions of words, encompassing books, articles, websites, and countless other sources. This scale enables them to develop broad knowledge and flexible language capabilities that smaller models can't match. For sales professionals, large language models enable several practical applications.

Research and summarization. You can ask a large language model to summarize a company's recent earnings call, explain their competitive positioning, or identify themes across their public communications. The model synthesizes information and presents it in digestible form.

Writing assistance. Large language models draft emails, proposals, and other sales content. They adapt tone and style based on context. They personalize content based on recipient information. They overcome blank-page paralysis by providing starting points that salespeople can refine.

Question answering. Sales involves constant information needs. What's the competitive positioning against a specific rival? What objections typically arise for a particular product? What case studies are relevant for a given industry? Large language models can answer these questions by drawing on their training data and any additional context provided.

Conversation practice. Some organizations use large language models for role-playing exercises. Salespeople practice pitches, objection handling, and discovery conversations with an AI that simulates customer responses. This enables practice at scale without requiring manager time for every session.

The capabilities of large language models continue expanding rapidly. Sales applications that seem cutting-edge today will likely become standard features in mainstream sales platforms within a few years.

Connecting Technology to Sales Applications

Abstract understanding of AI technology becomes useful when connected to specific sales applications. Here's how the technologies map to tools you'll encounter.

Lead scoring platforms typically use supervised machine learning to analyze historical conversion data and predict which new leads are most likely to convert. The better platforms incorporate diverse data sources: firmographic information, behavioral signals, engagement patterns, and third-party intent data. Questions to ask vendors: What data trains your model? How often is it retrained? How do you handle new customers who lack historical data?

Conversation intelligence tools combine speech recognition to transcribe calls with NLP to analyze content. They identify key moments, track metrics like talk-time ratio, and flag coaching opportunities. Advanced platforms use neural networks to detect sentiment and emotion beyond word-level analysis. Questions to ask: How accurate is transcription across accents and audio quality? What specific insights does the analysis provide? How do insights connect to coaching recommendations?

Email automation platforms use NLP for personalization and optimization. They analyze recipient characteristics to tailor messaging, predict optimal send times, and suggest subject lines likely to drive opens. Some incorporate language generation to draft content. Questions to ask: What level of personalization does the system actually provide? How are send times optimized? What data shows the system improves results?

Sales forecasting tools apply predictive analytics to pipeline data. They consider deal characteristics, historical patterns, and often incorporate signals that salespeople might not track manually. The best systems explain their predictions rather than just providing numbers. Questions to ask: What factors does the model consider? How accurate has forecasting been historically? How do predictions change as deals progress?

AI assistants and copilots leverage large language models to provide general-purpose support. They can research prospects, draft communications, answer questions, and help with various tasks that benefit from language understanding and generation. Questions to ask: What data does the assistant have access to? How does it handle confidential information? What are the limits of its knowledge?

The questions suggested for each category share a common theme: understanding what's actually happening beneath the marketing claims. Vendors will promise AI-powered everything. Your job is determining whether the AI delivers genuine value for your specific situation. The conceptual foundation from this chapter equips you to have those conversations with confidence. You don't need to understand every technical detail, but you do need to know enough to separate tools that will transform your work from those that will waste your budget.

Evaluating AI Tools

Armed with foundational understanding, you can evaluate AI tools more effectively. Several questions cut through marketing language to reveal actual capability.

What training data underlies the system? AI is only as good as the data it learns from. A lead scoring model trained on data from a different industry or company size may not transfer to your context. Ask vendors where their training data comes from, how much they have, and how relevant it is to your situation.

How does the system handle edge cases? AI systems perform well on typical cases similar to their training data. They often struggle with unusual situations. Ask vendors what happens when the system encounters something it hasn't seen before. Does it fail gracefully? Does it flag uncertainty? Or does it produce confident but unreliable outputs?

What does the system actually automate versus augment? Marketing materials often blur the line between AI that handles tasks independently and AI that assists human judgment. Clarify what the system does on its own versus what it recommends for human decision. The distinction matters for how you'll integrate the tool into your workflow.

Can you explain the outputs? Black-box predictions have limited usefulness if you can't understand why the system reached its conclusions. Some tools provide explanations alongside predictions. Others offer only numbers. If you want to learn from AI insights rather than just follow them, explainability matters.

What happens when the AI is wrong? Every AI system makes mistakes. The question is how you'll know when it's wrong and what the consequences will be. Ask vendors about error rates, how errors are detected, and what safeguards exist against acting on incorrect outputs.

How does the system improve over time? AI systems should improve as they accumulate more data and feedback. Ask vendors how their systems learn from outcomes in your environment. Do they retrain on your data? How often? What happens if your business changes?

These questions won't make you popular with vendors who prefer to demo features rather than discuss limitations. Ask them anyway. The time invested in rigorous evaluation pays off in tools that actually deliver value rather than tools that looked impressive in a sales presentation. Vendors who can answer these questions confidently have built systems worth considering. Vendors who deflect or offer vague assurances are selling promises rather than proven capability. Your goal isn't to find the most sophisticated AI. It's to find AI that works reliably in your specific context, and these questions reveal whether a tool meets that standard.

Recognizing AI Theater

Not everything marketed as AI deserves the label. Some vendors apply "AI" to systems that use simple rules, basic statistics, or minimal automation. This AI theater proliferates because the term drives buyer interest. Recognizing it protects you from wasted investment.

Several red flags suggest a tool isn't delivering genuine AI capability. Vague explanations top the list. Legitimate AI vendors can explain, at least conceptually, how their systems work. If a vendor can't articulate what type of AI they use or what data trains their models, skepticism is warranted. Another warning sign is the absence of learning from data. True AI improves as it processes more information. If a system produces the same outputs regardless of how much data it has, it's probably rules in disguise. Similarly, watch for identical recommendations across contexts. AI should recognize differences between situations and tailor its outputs accordingly. If the system gives the same recommendations to every user regardless of their specific circumstances, it's not doing the pattern recognition that defines AI.

Be wary of vendors who avoid measuring results. Those confident in their systems track outcomes and share data on effectiveness. Vendors who sidestep discussions about results may be hiding weak performance. Finally, ask whether humans are doing the work behind the scenes. Some "AI" services actually rely on human workers processing requests manually, at least for complex cases. This isn't necessarily bad, but it's not AI. Ask vendors directly whether humans are involved in producing outputs.

The Appropriate Level of Trust

AI systems deserve neither blind faith nor reflexive skepticism. They're tools with specific strengths and limitations. Calibrating your trust appropriately requires understanding both. AI tends to perform well when tasks involve pattern recognition across large datasets, when good training data is available, when the future resembles the past, and when mistakes are recoverable. Lead scoring fits these criteria well. Historical data is abundant, patterns are relatively stable, and acting on a bad score has limited consequences.

AI tends to struggle when tasks require understanding context not present in the data, when situations differ substantially from training examples, when common sense matters, and when the environment is changing rapidly. Negotiating a complex enterprise deal involves contextual factors, unique stakeholder dynamics, and judgment calls that AI isn't equipped to handle independently. Practical trust calibration means relying on AI more heavily for tasks where it excels and maintaining human judgment for tasks where it struggles. It means using AI predictions as inputs to decisions rather than substitutes for decisions. It means staying alert for situations where AI outputs don't seem right and investigating rather than overriding your instincts automatically.

The salespeople who use AI most effectively treat it as a capable but imperfect colleague. They value its contributions without abdicating their own judgment. They learn its tendencies and adjust their reliance accordingly. They recognize that the combination of human and AI judgment typically outperforms either alone.

Staying Current Without Drowning

AI capabilities are evolving quickly. The tools available today will be superseded by more powerful tools within a few years. For sales professionals, this creates a challenge: how do you stay current without becoming overwhelmed by constant technology shifts? Several strategies help.

Focus on capabilities rather than products. Specific tools will come and go. The underlying capabilities, like predictive lead scoring or conversation intelligence, persist across product generations. Understanding what AI can do for sales matters more than mastering any particular tool.

Learn through application. Abstract study of AI trends produces limited retention. Learning happens faster when you're applying tools to real sales challenges. Start using AI tools for actual work, and your understanding will develop through practice.

Build evaluation skills. The ability to assess new tools quickly matters more than deep expertise in current tools. Develop your ability to ask good questions, run meaningful tests, and determine whether a tool delivers real value for your situation.

Maintain perspective. AI is a tool, not a religion. The goal isn't adopting AI for its own sake. The goal is selling more effectively. Not every AI tool will improve your results. Not every AI trend will matter for your work. Focus on applications that address actual bottlenecks in your sales process.

Accept imperfect knowledge. You won't understand every technical detail of the AI systems you use. That's fine. Pilots don't fully understand the physics of flight. Surgeons don't fully understand the chemistry of anesthesia. Effective use doesn't require complete understanding. It requires enough understanding to make good decisions.

Preparing for What Comes Next

The fundamentals covered in this chapter provide a foundation for the applications explored in subsequent chapters. Machine learning, neural networks, NLP, predictive analytics, and large language models power the specific tools we'll examine. That examination begins with prospecting. Finding the right prospects has always consumed significant sales effort. It's also where AI has delivered some of the most measurable impact. The next chapter explores how AI transforms the work of identifying, prioritizing, and targeting potential customers, and how you can apply these capabilities to fill your pipeline with better opportunities.

Chapter Three

Finding the Right Prospects

The Numbers Game Reconsidered

Sales has always been a numbers game. Make more calls, send more emails, knock on more doors, and eventually you'll find buyers. This approach isn't wrong. Activity matters. But it's incomplete in ways that become increasingly costly as markets grow more competitive. The flaw in pure volume approaches is that not all prospects are equal. Some will never buy regardless of how well you sell. Their budgets don't exist. Their needs don't align. Their organizations aren't ready. Pursuing these prospects consumes time that could go toward better opportunities. The salesperson who makes a hundred calls to unqualified prospects loses to the salesperson who makes fifty calls to qualified ones.

AI changes the math of prospecting. Instead of treating all potential contacts as roughly equivalent, AI identifies which prospects are most likely to buy. It analyzes patterns across vast datasets to predict fit and readiness. It monitors behavioral signals that indicate buying intent. It enables salespeople to focus their finite time on opportunities with the highest probability of success. This shift from volume to precision doesn't eliminate the importance of activity. It multiplies the return on activity. The same effort applied to better-targeted prospects produces more pipeline, more closed deals, and more revenue. Understanding how AI enables this targeting is essential for modern sales effectiveness.

Predictive Lead Scoring

Traditional lead scoring assigns points based on predetermined criteria. A lead in your target industry gets ten points. A director-level title adds fifteen. Visiting the pricing page contributes twenty. Marketing sets these rules based on assumptions about what matters. Leads exceeding a threshold score pass to sales.

This approach has limitations. The rules reflect human assumptions that may be wrong. They don't adapt as markets change. They can't capture complex interactions between factors. A lead might score highly on individual criteria but still be a poor fit because of combinations the scoring rules don't address. Predictive lead scoring applies machine learning to overcome these limitations. Instead of following predetermined rules, the system analyzes historical data about leads that converted versus those that didn't. It identifies patterns that distinguish winners from losers, including patterns that humans never specified or even recognized.

The practical difference is substantial. A B2B software company implemented predictive lead scoring and discovered that their traditional scoring model was systematically wrong. Their rules emphasized company size, but the data showed that mid-sized companies in growth phases converted at much higher rates than large enterprises, regardless of other factors. Their rules awarded points for whitepaper downloads, but the data revealed that webinar attendance was actually a stronger indicator. The predictive model captured these realities. Conversion rates from scored leads increased by thirty-four percent.

Predictive scoring also handles complexity that rule-based systems can't match. The signal value of a pricing page visit might depend on how long the visitor stayed, what pages they viewed before and after, whether they've visited before, and what their company's current technology stack looks like. Machine learning models consider these interactions automatically. Writing rules to cover all relevant combinations would be impossible. For salespeople, predictive scoring means prioritization you can trust. When the system says this lead deserves attention, that recommendation rests on statistical patterns drawn from thousands of similar cases. It doesn't guarantee conversion. Nothing does. But it significantly improves your odds of spending time on opportunities that go somewhere.

Intent Data: Signals of Readiness

Not every well-fitted prospect is ready to buy. Timing matters as much as fit. A company might be a perfect candidate for your solution but have just signed a three-year contract with a competitor. Pursuing them now wastes effort better spent elsewhere. Intent data addresses timing by identifying prospects actively researching solutions like yours. These signals come from multiple sources, each revealing different dimensions of buying readiness.

First-party intent captures behavior on your own properties. When a prospect visits your website, downloads content, attends webinars, or engages with emails, these actions signal interest. Modern tracking provides detailed visibility: which pages they viewed, how long they spent, what they searched for, and how their engagement compares to typical buying patterns. Third-party intent extends this view beyond your properties. Specialized data providers monitor activity across publisher networks, review sites, and research platforms. When companies research topics related to your solution, even if they've never visited your site, intent data providers can identify them. A prospect reading analyst reports about your product category, visiting competitor websites, and searching for relevant keywords is signaling buying interest. Technographic intent adds another layer by identifying technology changes that create buying opportunities. When a company adds or removes specific technologies from their stack, it often indicates broader initiatives that your solution might support. A company implementing a new CRM might also need sales enablement tools. A company adopting cloud infrastructure might need security solutions. The power of intent data comes from combining signals across sources. First-party engagement plus third-party research activity plus relevant technology changes creates a composite picture of readiness that no single signal provides.

Rachel sells marketing automation software. Her AI-powered prospecting platform combines intent signals to generate a daily priority list. One morning, the system flagged a manufacturing company she'd never contacted. The signals: they had visited her company's website three times in two weeks, their marketing director had downloaded an industry report from a third-party research site, and they had recently implemented a new CRM that integrates with her platform. She called that afternoon. The marketing director admitted they were starting a vendor evaluation and hadn't yet reached out to anyone. Rachel entered the conversation before competitors knew an opportunity existed.

Pattern Recognition Across Data Sources

Individual data points tell limited stories. Pattern recognition across multiple data sources reveals insights that no single source provides. Consider what AI can synthesize about a prospect. From the company's website: their messaging, priorities, and recent announcements. From financial data: their revenue trajectory, profitability, and investment patterns. From job postings: what capabilities they're building and what challenges they might be facing. From news coverage: executive changes, strategic initiatives, and market pressures. From social media: what their leaders are discussing and endorsing. From technographic databases: what systems they use and what gaps might exist. From intent signals: what they're researching and when.

Human salespeople could theoretically analyze all these sources for every prospect. In practice, time constraints make comprehensive research impossible for more than a handful of priority accounts. AI processes this information at scale, synthesizing patterns that would take hours to identify manually. The patterns that matter extend beyond individual prospects to market-level insights. AI can identify that companies in a specific industry vertical are showing elevated interest in a particular category. It can detect that prospects with certain characteristics tend to become customers when they exhibit a specific sequence of behaviors. It can recognize emerging trends before they're obvious. These market-level patterns inform prospecting strategy, not just individual targeting. If AI detects growing interest from a vertical you haven't prioritized, that insight shapes where you focus development efforts. If a new buying signal emerges that wasn't previously significant, you want to know.

Building Your Ideal Customer Profile

AI doesn't replace the need for an ideal customer profile. It sharpens that profile by testing assumptions against data. Most sales organizations have some version of an ideal customer profile: the characteristics that define companies most likely to buy and succeed with the product. These profiles typically rest on experience and intuition. We sell well to mid-sized technology companies. Healthcare enterprises have long sales cycles. Financial services prospects care most about security.

AI validates or challenges these assumptions. Analysis of historical deal data might confirm that mid-sized technology companies convert well, but it might also reveal that a specific subsegment of manufacturing companies converts even better despite receiving less attention. The profile expands based on evidence rather than limiting itself to established assumptions. The validation process surfaces non-obvious characteristics that matter. Standard profiles focus on firmographics: industry, company size, geography, and revenue. AI analysis might reveal that growth rate matters more than absolute size, that companies with specific technology stacks are better fits, or that certain hiring patterns predict buying readiness. These insights refine targeting beyond conventional dimensions.

A cybersecurity firm discovered through AI analysis that their ideal customer profile was significantly wrong. Their salespeople had always prioritized financial services companies, which seemed like natural buyers for security solutions. Data analysis revealed that these companies had the longest sales cycles, highest acquisition costs, and lowest lifetime value in their portfolio. Healthcare organizations with between two hundred and five hundred employees, a segment they had largely ignored, showed dramatically better metrics across every dimension. They shifted prospecting focus accordingly. Pipeline efficiency improved within two quarters.

Implementing AI-Powered Prospecting

Moving from traditional prospecting to AI-powered prospecting requires thoughtful implementation. Several principles guide successful transitions. Start with data quality, because AI systems produce outputs only as good as their inputs. If your CRM contains outdated information, duplicate records, and inconsistent data entry, AI analysis will reflect those problems. Before implementing sophisticated prospecting tools, invest in cleaning and standardizing your existing data. Establish processes that maintain quality going forward. From there, focus on integrating data sources. AI prospecting works best when it can access diverse information. First-party engagement data, third-party intent signals, firmographic information, and technographic data each contribute to accurate targeting. The more signals available, the more patterns AI can identify. Evaluate what data sources you currently use, what additional sources might be valuable, and how to connect them.

When you first implement AI prospecting tools, trust but verify. Run parallel processes. Follow the AI recommendations, but also maintain some traditional prospecting to compare results. This verification period builds confidence in the system and surfaces any calibration issues. Once you've confirmed that AI recommendations outperform alternatives, shift reliance accordingly. Throughout implementation, feed outcomes back into the system. AI prospecting improves through feedback loops. When recommended leads convert, that confirms the patterns the system identified. When they don't convert, that provides information for refinement. Ensure your processes capture outcomes and that this data flows back to the AI system. Prospecting accuracy improves over time as the system learns from results. Most importantly, maintain human judgment in the loop. AI prospecting identifies statistically likely opportunities. It doesn't guarantee that every recommendation makes sense. Salespeople should review AI suggestions with their own judgment about fit, timing, and strategic priorities. The best results come from AI pattern recognition combined with human contextual understanding.

The Over-Reliance Trap

AI prospecting tools are powerful. That power creates risk of over-reliance. The risk manifests in several ways. Salespeople might stop exercising their own judgment about prospect fit, deferring entirely to system scores. They might ignore opportunities that don't score highly even when contextual factors suggest potential. They might lose the prospecting skills they'll need if systems fail or change. Consider what happens when AI scoring misses. The system was trained on historical patterns, but markets evolve. A new vertical might emerge that doesn't resemble past successful customers. A shift in buyer behavior might invalidate previous signals. A novel use case might attract prospects with characteristics the model has never seen. Over-reliance on AI scoring in these situations causes salespeople to miss opportunities that judgment would catch.

The solution isn't avoiding AI prospecting. It's maintaining balance. Use AI recommendations as a primary input while preserving the habit of independent evaluation. Question scores that don't match your instincts. Stay alert for patterns the system might be missing. Treat AI as a highly capable research assistant rather than an infallible oracle. Organizations should also design processes that prevent over-reliance. Allocate some prospecting time to exploratory outreach beyond AI recommendations. Review deals that succeeded despite low AI scores to understand what signals the system missed. Create feedback mechanisms that capture salesperson insights about why recommendations did or didn't pan out.

Human Judgment in Prospect Selection

Certain prospecting decisions require human judgment that AI can't provide. Strategic fit assessment is one such area. AI identifies prospects likely to buy based on patterns, but it doesn't assess whether those prospects align with strategic priorities. A company might be an excellent fit for your current product but a poor match for where you're heading. A prospect might be ready to buy a small deal but incapable of growing into a significant account. These strategic considerations require human evaluation. Relationship and access factors represent another blind spot for AI. The system doesn't know that your board member's former colleague is now CEO at a target company. It doesn't recognize that a prospect's company just hired someone from your largest customer who could be an internal advocate. These relationship and access factors significantly influence deal probability. Salespeople should overlay this knowledge on AI recommendations.

Competitive dynamics also require human insight. AI prospecting typically focuses on prospect characteristics and behavior. It may not account for competitive positioning in specific accounts. A prospect might show strong intent signals but be deeply embedded with a competitor in ways that make switching unlikely. Salespeople with competitive intelligence can adjust prioritization accordingly. Finally, ethical considerations belong to humans. Some prospects might be poor fits for reasons that matter but aren't captured in data. A company might be engaged in practices that conflict with your values. A deal might be winnable but likely to create problems. These judgment calls can't be delegated to algorithms. The best prospecting combines AI's analytical power with human judgment on factors machines can't evaluate. Neither alone matches what both provide together.

Outreach Timing and Sequencing

Identifying the right prospects is half the challenge. Reaching them at the right time with the right approach is the other half. AI contributes here as well. AI excels at optimal timing analysis, examining engagement patterns to identify when prospects are most likely to respond. For email, this might mean determining that a specific prospect tends to engage with messages sent on Tuesday mornings. For calls, it might mean recognizing patterns in when they answer versus when calls go to voicemail. Aggregate analysis across many prospects reveals timing patterns by segment, role, and other characteristics. Beyond general timing, AI enables trigger-based outreach by monitoring for events that create opportunities. A prospect company announces a relevant initiative. An executive at a target account changes roles. A competitor stumbles publicly. Intent signals spike. These triggers indicate moments when outreach is particularly likely to resonate. AI detection enables response faster than manual monitoring allows.

AI also contributes to sequence optimization, testing different combinations of emails, calls, and social touches to determine what works best for different prospect types. What order should those touches follow? With what spacing? AI measures response rates and identifies winning patterns. The salesperson follows optimized sequences rather than guessing about cadence. Throughout the sequence, AI helps with message personalization, determining not just when to reach out but what to say. Based on prospect characteristics, recent activity, and historical patterns, AI suggests messaging angles likely to resonate. A prospect researching a specific topic gets outreach addressing that topic. A prospect whose company just announced relevant news gets outreach referencing that news. These timing and sequencing capabilities multiply the impact of accurate prospect identification. Finding the right people matters less if you reach them at the wrong time with generic messaging.

Measuring Prospecting Effectiveness

AI enables more sophisticated measurement of prospecting performance. Traditional metrics like calls made and emails sent measure activity. AI-enhanced metrics measure effectiveness. Start with targeting accuracy: what percentage of prospects you contact ultimately convert? AI prospecting should improve this ratio. Track conversion rates from AI-recommended prospects versus other sources. If AI targeting isn't delivering measurably better results, something is wrong with the implementation. Time to pipeline offers another valuable measure, tracking how quickly prospects progress from initial contact to qualified opportunity. AI should reduce this time by identifying prospects who are closer to readiness. Measure velocity from first touch to opportunity creation.

Opportunity quality matters as much as quantity since not all pipeline is equal. AI prospecting should produce opportunities that close at higher rates and for larger values. Compare close rates and deal sizes from AI-sourced opportunities to other sources. Effort efficiency captures how many touches it takes to create an opportunity. AI should improve this ratio by focusing effort on more receptive prospects. Track touches per opportunity by source. Finally, don't overlook false negatives. AI scoring isn't just wrong when highly scored leads don't convert. It's also wrong when it gives low scores to leads that would have converted. This is harder to measure since you typically don't pursue low-scored leads. Periodically test low-scored cohorts to estimate what you might be missing. These metrics provide feedback for continuous improvement. They also create accountability for AI tool investments. If prospecting tools aren't delivering measurable improvement, reconsider the investment or the implementation.

Scaling Prospecting Without Losing Quality

One promise of AI prospecting is scale without proportional effort increase. This promise is real but requires intentional execution. The trap is letting volume overwhelm quality. AI can identify thousands of potential prospects. Pursuing all of them with minimal personalization produces worse results than pursuing fewer with genuine relevance. The goal isn't maximum volume. It's optimal volume at maintained quality.

Setting appropriate thresholds matters. Don't pursue every prospect that clears a minimum score. Focus on the highest-potential opportunities that your capacity can handle well. It's better to engage two hundred prospects with thoughtful outreach than a thousand prospects with generic messaging. Tiered approaches help manage scale. Highest-potential prospects receive the most personalized treatment: custom research, tailored messaging, and sustained attention. Mid-tier prospects receive semi-personalized outreach: templated but customized for key characteristics. Lower tiers receive standardized nurture sequences until their signals strengthen. AI helps sort prospects into appropriate tiers and enables personalization at each level.

Automation should support quality, not undermine it. Automated outreach sequences make sense for prospects who aren't ready for direct engagement. Once a prospect signals readiness, human attention should take over. The handoff point matters. Automating too long damages relationships. Transitioning too early wastes human capacity.

Looking Beyond Initial Contact

AI prospecting isn't just about identifying who to contact first. It's about understanding prospects deeply enough to engage them effectively throughout the sales process. The intelligence gathered during prospecting informs later conversations. What challenges is the company facing? What initiatives are they pursuing? What priorities do their executives discuss publicly? What technology decisions have they made? AI surfaces this information at scale. Salespeople who internalize it enter conversations with context that generic competitors lack.

This sets up the next stage of the sales process: understanding your customer deeply enough to serve them well. Prospecting identifies who to pursue. Customer understanding determines whether you can actually help them and how to communicate that value. The next chapter explores how AI enhances the depth of customer understanding throughout the sales relationship.

Chapter Four

Understanding Your Customer

Beyond Surface-Level Knowledge

Every salesperson knows that understanding customers matters. The question is what understanding actually means and how deep it goes. Surface-level knowledge includes the basics: company name, industry, size, and the contact's title. Most salespeople capture this information. It's table stakes, not advantage. Competitors have the same facts from the same sources. Deeper understanding involves knowing what customers actually care about, what pressures they face, what outcomes they need, and what concerns they haven't voiced. This understanding enables salespeople to position solutions in terms that resonate, anticipate objections before they arise, and provide value beyond the transaction. The salespeople who consistently win competitive deals typically possess this deeper understanding.

The challenge has always been scale. Deep understanding takes time to develop. You can't research every prospect thoroughly. You can't remember every detail from past conversations. You can't track every signal across every account. Human cognitive limits create a ceiling on how many customers you can truly understand. AI raises that ceiling. It processes signals that humans miss, remembers details that humans forget, and identifies patterns across interactions that no individual could track. The result isn't surveillance for its own sake. It's genuine insight that helps salespeople serve customers better. Understanding AI's role in customer insight, and its appropriate boundaries, makes the difference between using these capabilities well and using them poorly.

What AI Sees That Humans Miss

Human perception has limits. We can only process so much information at once. We notice what we're looking for and miss what we're not. We remember selectively, often forgetting details that turn out to matter. We struggle to detect gradual changes even when sudden changes are obvious. AI doesn't share these limits. It processes comprehensive information without selective attention. It retains complete records without memory decay. It detects subtle patterns across time that would be invisible to human observation.

Consider what happens during a sales call. A skilled salesperson pays attention to what the customer says, asks follow-up questions, and tries to read between the lines. But even the best salesperson can only focus on so much. While listening to the customer's words, they might miss subtle shifts in tone. While formulating the next question, they might not fully register hesitation in the customer's voice. While managing the conversation flow, they might not track exactly how much time they've spent talking versus listening. AI conversation tools capture everything simultaneously. They track the words spoken, the tone used, the pace of speech, the interruptions that occurred, and the silences that preceded certain topics. They identify when customers sound engaged versus uncertain, when they're leaning in versus pulling back. They notice patterns a human couldn't: this customer always hesitates before discussing budget, or their energy drops whenever implementation timelines come up.

This comprehensive perception applies across all customer touchpoints, not just conversations. AI tracks which emails customers open, which links they click, which pages they visit, and how their engagement patterns change over time. It notices when a customer who previously responded within hours starts taking days. It detects when website visits shift from educational content to comparison pages. These signals combine into a picture of customer state that no human could assemble manually.

Conversation Intelligence in Practice

Conversation intelligence platforms transform how salespeople learn from customer interactions. These systems record calls and meetings, transcribe them automatically, and analyze the content for insights. The transcription alone provides value. Salespeople no longer rely on notes taken during conversations, which are always incomplete and sometimes wrong. They have complete records they can search, reference, and share. When preparing for a follow-up meeting, they can review exactly what was discussed previously rather than working from memory.

But analysis goes further than transcription. Modern conversation intelligence extracts structured data from unstructured conversations. Topic tracking identifies what subjects came up and how much time was spent on each. Did you spend most of the call discussing features while the customer wanted to talk about implementation? The data shows the imbalance. Did pricing come up early or late in the conversation? The timing might indicate how central cost concerns are to their decision. Question analysis examines the questions asked and answered. Effective discovery depends on asking good questions, and AI can assess question quality: Are you asking open-ended questions that encourage customer elaboration? Are you following up on important topics or moving on too quickly? Are you asking about business outcomes or just product requirements?

Talk-time ratios measure who dominated the conversation. Top performers typically listen more than they talk, especially in discovery calls. If you're speaking seventy percent of the time, you're not learning enough about the customer's situation. Conversation intelligence provides exact measurements that enable adjustment. Sentiment tracking assesses emotional tone throughout the conversation, revealing when the customer sounded most engaged, when they seemed uncertain or skeptical, and whether there were moments when energy dropped. These emotional contours reveal what matters to the customer beyond their explicit statements. The platforms also excel at key moment identification, flagging specific points that deserve attention: a customer mentions a competitor, a decision-maker expresses concern about a specific issue, a stakeholder asks for something outside normal scope. AI identifies these moments so salespeople and managers can focus review time on what matters most.

Thomas manages a team of eight enterprise account executives. Before implementing conversation intelligence, his coaching depended on ride-alongs and self-reports. He could observe maybe two calls per rep per month. Now he reviews AI-flagged moments from dozens of calls weekly. He spotted a pattern: one rep consistently talked past customer objections without acknowledging them. That specific behavior wasn't visible in summary metrics. It was visible in conversation analysis. Targeted coaching addressed the pattern. The rep's close rate improved within a quarter.

Decoding Customer Sentiment

Customers don't always say what they mean. They express polite interest when they're not interested at all. They voice mild concerns when they have major objections. They say "we'll think about it" when they've already decided no. Reading the emotional reality beneath the surface has always distinguished top salespeople. AI sentiment analysis brings scale and consistency to this reading. Modern NLP models assess emotional tone with increasing accuracy, identifying not just positive and negative sentiment but more nuanced states like uncertainty, frustration, enthusiasm, and hesitation.

Email analysis provides one application. A customer's messages might be polite and professional while containing subtle signals of disengagement. Response times lengthen. Messages become shorter. Specific questions get vague answers. Individual changes are easy to miss. AI tracking detects the cumulative pattern and flags accounts where sentiment appears to be shifting. Social monitoring extends sentiment analysis beyond direct communications. What are customers saying about your company, your product category, or relevant topics on social platforms? What are their executives posting about industry challenges? This public sentiment data adds context to direct interactions.

The real power emerges from combining sentiment sources. A customer who expresses enthusiasm in calls but whose email responsiveness is declining presents a different picture than sentiment analysis of either channel alone would suggest. Perhaps they're personally supportive but facing internal resistance. Perhaps they're managing stakeholder concerns they haven't shared directly. The combined view prompts the salesperson to probe in ways that single-channel analysis wouldn't suggest.

Sentiment analysis isn't mind reading. It's pattern recognition that supplements human judgment. The salesperson still interprets what signals mean and decides how to respond. AI provides data that would otherwise be unavailable or too scattered to aggregate.

Digital Body Language

In face-to-face interactions, body language communicates as much as words. Leaning in signals engagement. Crossed arms suggest resistance. Eye contact indicates attention. Salespeople learn to read these cues and adjust accordingly. Digital interactions lack physical presence but generate their own behavioral signals. These signals constitute digital body language: the patterns of online behavior that reveal customer state.

Engagement depth measures how customers interact with your content and communications. A prospect who spends fifteen minutes on a case study page is signaling something different than one who bounces after ten seconds. A customer who watches an entire product video to the end has different interest than one who abandons at the thirty-second mark. Email opens matter less than email clicks, which matter less than time spent on the linked content. Navigation patterns reveal what customers are actually trying to accomplish. A prospect who goes directly to pricing after visiting the homepage has different intent than one who methodically works through feature pages. A customer who repeatedly returns to the same help article might be struggling with something they haven't reported. Movement through your digital properties tells a story about their needs and concerns.

Frequency changes indicate shifts in relationship state. A customer who historically logged in weekly but now logs in daily might be expanding usage. Or they might be troubleshooting problems. The change itself is a signal worth investigating. Decreased frequency often predicts churn before any explicit dissatisfaction appears. Timing patterns suggest urgency and priority. A prospect researching at midnight is signaling something different than one researching during business hours. A customer who starts checking competitor websites indicates active evaluation. A contact who suddenly engages with contract-related content after months of silence is sending a clear signal.

AI aggregates these behavioral signals across touchpoints, identifies significant patterns, and surfaces insights that inform sales engagement. The salesperson doesn't need to track all these signals manually. AI handles the monitoring and alerts when patterns warrant attention.

Mapping the Customer Journey

Individual signals gain meaning within the context of the customer journey. Where is this prospect in their buying process? What typically happens next? What concerns tend to arise at this stage? Journey context transforms isolated data points into actionable understanding. AI maps customer journeys by analyzing patterns across many customers. It identifies common paths from initial awareness through purchase decision. It detects when individual customers diverge from typical patterns. It predicts what actions and concerns are likely based on where customers are in their journey.

The journey view helps salespeople calibrate their approach. Early-stage prospects need education about problems and possibilities. Mid-stage prospects need comparison information and social proof. Late-stage prospects need confidence in implementation and outcomes. AI journey identification helps salespeople deliver the right content and conversations for each stage. Journey analysis also reveals bottlenecks and drop-off points. If prospects consistently stall at a particular stage, that indicates something about your sales process, your messaging, or your product that needs attention. If customers who engage with a specific piece of content progress faster, that content deserves more prominence. These insights emerge from pattern analysis across many journeys rather than intuition from individual cases.

An industrial equipment manufacturer analyzed their customer journey data and discovered an unexpected pattern. Prospects who visited the technical specifications page after the pricing page closed at much lower rates than those who visited pricing after specifications. The sequence mattered more than whether they visited either page. Further analysis suggested that spec-first visitors were qualifying the solution before considering cost, while price-first visitors were shopping on cost and often chose cheaper alternatives. The company adjusted their website navigation to encourage the higher-converting sequence. They also trained salespeople to recognize the pattern and adjust discovery conversations accordingly.

Predicting Customer Needs

Understanding current customer state is valuable. Predicting future needs is transformative. Predictive models analyze patterns to forecast what customers will want before they express it. The foundation is historical data about what customers with similar characteristics and behaviors eventually needed. When current customers match those patterns, predictions about their future needs follow.

These predictions take several forms. Upsell and cross-sell prediction identifies existing customers likely to need additional products or services. A customer whose usage patterns resemble other customers who eventually upgraded is probably a candidate for upgrade conversations. A customer whose industry typically purchases a complementary product, but who hasn't yet, might be receptive to that offering. Churn prediction identifies customers at risk of leaving before they've decided to leave. The signals often precede explicit dissatisfaction: declining usage, slower response times, decreased engagement with new features, increased support tickets. Early identification enables proactive intervention rather than reactive retention attempts.

Need timing prediction forecasts when customers will be ready for specific conversations. A customer might be a good candidate for a renewal conversation, but the timing isn't right yet. AI analysis of their behavior, contract cycles, and patterns from similar customers can suggest when to engage. Problem prediction anticipates issues customers are likely to experience. If customers with similar characteristics commonly encounter a specific challenge, proactive outreach about that challenge demonstrates understanding and provides value before problems escalate.

Kenji manages customer success for a SaaS company. His AI platform generates a daily list of accounts showing early warning signals. One customer appeared who had no open support tickets and no complaints in recent calls. But their usage patterns had shifted: fewer users logging in, shorter sessions, and no engagement with newly released features. He reached out for what he positioned as a standard check-in. The conversation revealed that a key champion had left the organization, and the remaining team was uncertain about the product's value. Without the early warning, he wouldn't have known to call until renewal conversations revealed the problem months later. With early warning, he had time to rebuild internal advocacy.

Integrating Multiple Data Streams

The full picture of customer understanding emerges from integrating data across sources. No single stream tells the complete story. AI integration creates comprehensive views that surpass what any individual source provides. CRM data provides the foundation: contact information, account history, deal stages, and logged interactions. This explicit data captures what salespeople and systems have recorded about the relationship. Marketing automation data adds engagement history: emails received and acted upon, content downloaded, webinars attended, and campaign responses. This shows how customers have interacted with your broader marketing efforts. Product usage data reveals how customers actually use what they've purchased: features adopted, frequency of use, patterns of engagement, and areas ignored. For software products especially, usage data provides insight into satisfaction and need that conversations might not surface.

Support data indicates where customers struggle: tickets opened, issues encountered, questions asked, and resolution patterns. Support interactions often reveal honest feedback that customers don't share in sales conversations. Financial data captures the economic relationship: purchase history, payment patterns, and revenue trends. Changes in purchasing behavior often signal relationship changes. External data adds context beyond your direct relationship: news about the customer's company, industry developments, competitive movements, and market conditions that might affect their needs. AI integration combines these streams into unified customer profiles. Rather than checking multiple systems to understand an account, salespeople access consolidated views that present relevant information in context. The integration surfaces signals that span systems: a customer whose support tickets increased while their product usage declined while their engagement with competitor content rose presents a coherent picture that isolated data wouldn't reveal.

The Ethics of Deep Understanding

Comprehensive customer intelligence raises ethical questions that deserve direct consideration. Where is the line between understanding customers to serve them better and surveilling customers in ways they wouldn't approve? Several principles guide ethical use. Purpose matters most. Intelligence gathering aimed at helping customers get better outcomes differs from intelligence gathering aimed at manipulation. Using sentiment analysis to identify when a customer needs support is appropriate. Using it to identify moments of weakness to pressure them is not. The test is whether the customer would feel served or exploited if they knew how their data was being used. Transparency builds trust in this context. Customers increasingly know that companies track their behavior. Pretending otherwise damages credibility. Being straightforward about what you track and why positions monitoring as service rather than surveillance. Many customers appreciate when salespeople reference their activity if it enables more relevant conversations.

Boundaries deserve respect as well. Some customer behavior happens in spaces where monitoring feels inappropriate. Tracking public social media posts is generally acceptable. Monitoring private communications that weren't shared with you isn't. The fact that something is technically possible to track doesn't mean it should be tracked. Value exchange applies here too. Customers accept data sharing when they receive value in return. If your customer intelligence enables genuinely better service, faster problem resolution, and more relevant recommendations, most customers accept the tradeoff. If it only benefits your sales efforts with no customer value, the exchange is unbalanced. Consent matters throughout. Explicit agreements about data use, even when legally optional, create clearer foundations for data-driven relationship management. Customers who knowingly opt into comprehensive service often become more comfortable with the practices that enable it. These principles don't eliminate all tension.

Competitive pressure pushes toward using every available advantage. Customer privacy concerns push toward restraint. Navigating this tension requires ongoing judgment rather than fixed rules.

Using Insights Effectively

Customer intelligence creates value only when it informs action. Having comprehensive data about an account matters little if salespeople don't know how to use it. Preparation improves dramatically with AI-synthesized intelligence. Before any customer interaction, salespeople can access more thorough preparation than manual research allows. What's happening in their business? What have they been researching? What topics emerged in previous conversations? What sentiment patterns have appeared? A few minutes reviewing AI-prepared briefings replaces hours of manual research while producing better results. This preparation elevates conversation quality. Salespeople who understand customer context ask better questions, make more relevant recommendations, and avoid topics that don't matter. They don't waste customer time on irrelevant discovery because they already know the basics. They probe deeper on issues that intelligence suggests are significant.

Intelligence also optimizes timing. Understanding customer journey stage, engagement patterns, and behavioral signals informs when to reach out and what to discuss. Rather than arbitrary check-ins, salespeople engage when signals suggest customers are ready for conversation. Personalization becomes genuine rather than performative. Generic references to "your industry challenges" feel hollow. Specific references to a customer's actual situation demonstrate understanding that builds credibility. Intelligence makes this specificity possible at scale. Perhaps most importantly, proactive service becomes possible. Rather than waiting for customers to report problems or express needs, salespeople anticipate and address them. This transforms the relationship from reactive support to proactive partnership. One caution: intelligence should inform conversations, not script them. Customers can tell when salespeople are reading from notes versus genuinely engaging. The goal is for intelligence to be internalized and natural, not recited and mechanical. Prepare thoroughly, then engage authentically.

Building Understanding Over Time

Customer understanding isn't a one-time achievement. It's a cumulative process that builds through the relationship. Early interactions provide limited data. You know what prospects tell you and what their public behavior reveals. As relationships develop, understanding deepens. You observe how they make decisions, what concerns recur, how they respond to different approaches. AI captures this learning and makes it accessible over time.

Institutional memory matters here. In organizations without AI-assisted intelligence, customer understanding often lives in individual salesperson heads. When people leave or accounts transfer, understanding evaporates. AI systems maintain comprehensive records that survive personnel changes. A new account manager can access the complete history of interactions, not just whatever the previous manager chose to document. Understanding also compounds across customers. Patterns learned from one customer inform expectations about similar customers. AI identifies these cross-customer patterns systematically. If customers in a particular industry commonly face a specific challenge, salespeople engaging new customers in that industry can anticipate and address it proactively. This compounding effect creates organizational advantage that grows over time. Companies that invest in customer intelligence build durable knowledge assets. Companies that don't repeatedly start from scratch.

From Understanding to Action

Deep customer understanding enables personalized engagement. Knowing what customers care about, where they are in their journey, and what needs they're likely to have creates the foundation for relevant, valuable interaction. But understanding without action is merely interesting. The next chapter examines how to translate customer understanding into personalized engagement at scale. AI enables not just knowing your customers better but serving them better through tailored messaging, relevant recommendations, and individualized experiences that feel personal without requiring proportional personal effort.

Chapter Five

Personalization at Scale

The Personalization Paradox

Sales effectiveness depends on relevance. Customers respond to salespeople who understand their specific situation, address their particular needs, and communicate in terms that resonate with their context. Generic pitches fail. Tailored engagement wins. This has always been true. The problem is math. Genuine personalization takes time. Understanding a prospect's business, crafting a message that speaks to their situation, and following up in contextually appropriate ways requires real effort. Multiply that effort by hundreds of prospects, and personalization becomes impossible to sustain. Salespeople face a choice: deep engagement with few prospects or shallow engagement with many.

This tradeoff has shaped sales strategy for decades. High-touch models assign salespeople to small territories where they can know every account intimately. High-volume models accept lower conversion rates in exchange for greater reach. Neither approach satisfies. The high-touch model limits scale. The high-volume model sacrifices effectiveness. AI dissolves this tradeoff. It enables personalization without proportional effort. What previously required hours of research and custom crafting can now happen in minutes with AI assistance. The result isn't just efficiency. It's a fundamental change in what's possible. Salespeople can deliver tailored engagement to larger audiences without degrading quality. The personalization paradox has a resolution.

What Personalization Actually Means

Before examining how AI enables personalization, we need clarity on what personalization involves. The term gets used loosely, sometimes to describe things that aren't genuinely personal at all. True personalization has several dimensions that work together to create communication that resonates. Relevance to situation means the communication addresses the recipient's actual circumstances, acknowledging their industry, company context, role challenges, and specific needs. Generic content that could apply to anyone isn't personalized regardless of how the recipient's name appears in the greeting. Appropriate timing matters just as much as what you say, because a perfectly crafted message sent at the wrong moment fails. Personalization includes adjusting when you engage based on individual readiness signals. Channel fit recognizes that different people prefer different communication methods. Some respond better to email, others prefer phone calls, and some engage through social platforms. Personalization means meeting people where they prefer to be met.

Tone and style matching acknowledges that communication style resonating with one person falls flat with another. Some prefer direct and efficient interaction while others want more relational warmth. Personalization adapts style to audience. Content depth calibration adjusts for the recipient's expertise and interests. Technical buyers want technical detail. Business buyers want business outcomes. Expert audiences need different content than novice audiences. Personalization adjusts content complexity and focus for the recipient. Each dimension requires knowledge about the individual recipient. That knowledge can come from research, from interaction history, from behavioral signals, or from inference based on characteristics. AI contributes to all of these sources, making comprehensive personalization achievable at scale.

Dynamic Content Assembly

The most direct AI application for personalization is dynamic content assembly. Rather than crafting each communication from scratch, salespeople start with components that AI assembles and customizes for specific recipients. Consider email outreach. A traditional personalized email requires the salesperson to research the prospect, identify relevant angles, write custom content, and review before sending. With AI assistance, the process transforms. The system accesses prospect data, selects relevant messaging components, customizes them for the specific situation, and generates a draft for review. The salesperson edits and approves rather than creates from nothing. The components that get assembled span the entire communication. Opening hooks get tailored to the recipient's situation, with AI referencing their company's recent announcement, their industry's current challenges, or a connection point relevant to their role. The hook draws on data about the specific recipient rather than generic category-level content. Value propositions get framed in terms the recipient cares about, recognizing that the same product feature can be positioned as cost savings for a CFO, efficiency gains for an operations leader, or competitive advantage for a CEO. AI selects and frames propositions based on recipient role and apparent priorities.

Social proof gets matched to the recipient's context because case studies and testimonials from companies similar to the prospect carry more weight than generic references. AI matches available proof points to recipient characteristics like industry, company size, and use case. Calls to action get calibrated to the recipient's journey stage, with early-stage prospects receiving invitations to educational content, mid-stage prospects receiving comparison tools, and late-stage prospects receiving proposal discussions. Even formatting and length get suited to the recipient's preferences. If behavioral data suggests a prospect engages with shorter messages, AI generates concise communication. If they tend to read longer content, AI provides more detail. The assembled result reads as a cohesive, personalized message rather than an obvious patchwork of components. Modern language models excel at producing natural-sounding output that integrates elements seamlessly.

Scaling Without Losing Soul

The efficiency of AI-powered personalization creates temptation. If AI can produce fifty personalized emails in the time it previously took to write five, why not send fifty? The math seems compelling. More personalized outreach should produce more results. This reasoning misses something important. Recipients can tell when communication is genuinely personal versus mechanically customized. The difference isn't always obvious in any single message. It becomes clear over the course of an interaction. If every message feels like it was assembled from a template, regardless of how well-customized, trust erodes.

Authenticity requires human involvement in the personalization process. AI should assist personalization, not fully automate it. The salesperson's role shifts from writing to editing, from creating to refining, from starting with blank pages to starting with intelligent drafts. But the role doesn't disappear. Several practices preserve authenticity while gaining AI efficiency. Every AI-generated message should pass through human review. Catch awkward phrasing. Add genuinely personal touches. Remove anything that feels off. The few minutes this takes are worth the authenticity preserved. Beyond review, salespeople should add human insight that AI can't access. AI knows what data reveals. Humans know things that aren't in data: a conversation detail, a mutual connection, an intuition about what the prospect cares about. Adding these human elements distinguishes communication that could have come from anyone using the same AI from communication that came from a specific person paying attention.

When stakes rise, human attention should increase proportionally. AI can handle routine communication efficiently, but a prospect expressing serious interest deserves direct human engagement, not an AI-assisted response that's slightly more customized than usual. Throughout this process, monitor recipient response. If response rates decline despite theoretically improved personalization, something is wrong. Either AI personalization isn't as good as expected, or recipients are detecting and rejecting automated engagement. Response data provides feedback for calibration. The goal isn't maximum automation. It's optimal automation. Find the level of AI assistance that improves efficiency while maintaining the human connection that makes sales relationships work.

Message Optimization and Testing

Personalization isn't just about tailoring content to individuals. It's also about improving what content works in general. AI enables systematic testing and optimization that improves messaging across the board. Subject line optimization tests which subject lines drive opens for different audience segments. AI generates variants, distributes them across similar prospects, measures results, and identifies what works. Over time, patterns emerge about what language, length, and approaches resonate with specific audiences. Send time optimization determines when messages are most likely to get response, analyzing engagement patterns by recipient, segment, and other variables. It identifies not just general best times but individual recipient preferences based on their historical behavior.

Sequence optimization tests entire outreach sequences rather than individual messages. Does a three-email sequence outperform a five-email sequence for certain prospect types? Should the second touch emphasize different value propositions than the first? AI tests alternatives and identifies winning combinations. Channel optimization determines which channels work best for different audiences, since some segments respond better to email, others to phone, and others to social touches. AI tracks cross-channel patterns and recommends optimal channel strategies by segment. The optimization process is continuous. Markets change. Recipient preferences evolve. What worked last quarter may not work next quarter. AI testing keeps messaging current rather than allowing it to drift toward stale approaches.

Elena manages marketing operations for a software company. Her team implemented AI-powered email optimization and discovered their assumptions about effective messaging were largely wrong. They had believed that subject lines referencing industry challenges outperformed those referencing product benefits. Testing showed the opposite for their primary segments. They had assumed longer emails with more detail would work better for technical buyers. Testing revealed that technical buyers responded better to concise emails that linked to detailed resources. Each discovery improved performance. Within six months, email response rates had increased by forty percent, not through better personalization alone but through better understanding of what personalized content should contain.

Recommendation Engines in Sales

Recommendation engines power much of modern e-commerce. Amazon's "customers who bought this also bought" and Netflix's "because you watched" features drive significant engagement and revenue. Similar technology applies in B2B sales contexts. Product recommendations identify which additional offerings are most relevant for specific customers. Based on what a customer has purchased, how they use it, and patterns from similar customers, AI recommends what else they're likely to need. This informs upsell and cross-sell conversations with suggestions tailored to each account. Content recommendations suggest which educational resources, case studies, and marketing materials are most relevant for each prospect. Rather than sending generic nurture content to everyone, AI matches content to individual interests and journey stages. A prospect researching a specific use case receives content about that use case. A prospect comparing alternatives receives comparison resources.

Action recommendations guide salespeople on what to do next with each opportunity. Given the current deal state, customer behavior, and patterns from similar deals, what action is most likely to advance the opportunity? AI recommendations help salespeople prioritize and choose effective next steps. Resource recommendations suggest which internal experts, reference customers, or supporting materials are most relevant for specific deals. A prospect with particular technical concerns might benefit from connecting with a solutions architect. A prospect in a specific industry might respond well to a reference from a peer company. AI matches resources to needs. These recommendation capabilities transform how salespeople operate. Instead of relying solely on personal judgment about what each customer needs, they receive AI-informed suggestions based on pattern analysis across many similar situations.

Personalized Pricing and Proposals

Pricing and proposal creation offer significant personalization opportunities that many organizations underutilize. Pricing personalization doesn't mean discriminatory pricing that charges different customers different amounts for identical offerings. It means structuring deals in ways that align with what specific customers value. The same total price can be packaged in various ways: upfront versus spread over time, per-user versus flat rate, bundled versus modular. Different structures appeal to different buyers based on their business models, budget constraints, and procurement preferences. AI analyzes historical deal data to identify which pricing structures succeed with different customer types. A customer whose characteristics match previous customers who preferred annual prepayment might receive proposals structured that way. A customer resembling those who needed monthly billing flexibility might receive different structure. The tailoring isn't arbitrary. It's pattern-based.

Proposal content benefits from similar personalization. Proposals typically contain multiple sections: executive summary, solution description, implementation approach, pricing, and terms. Each section can be customized based on what matters to the specific prospect. An executive summary for a CFO emphasizes different points than one for a CTO. A solution description for an enterprise buyer includes different detail than one for a mid-market buyer. Implementation sections should address the specific concerns and constraints the prospect has expressed. AI-assisted proposal generation enables this customization without requiring salespeople to rewrite proposals from scratch for every opportunity. Marcus sells enterprise software to healthcare organizations. His proposal process used to take hours per deal because healthcare buyers have specific compliance requirements that standard proposals didn't address. With AI-assisted proposal generation, the system knows that healthcare prospects need certain regulatory language, specific security attestations, and implementation approaches that account for industry constraints. Proposals generate with these elements included automatically. What took four hours now takes forty-five minutes. More importantly, prospects receive proposals that feel tailored to their world rather than generic documents they have to mentally translate.

The Uncanny Valley of Personalization

There's a phenomenon in robotics called the uncanny valley. As robots become more humanlike, people respond increasingly positively until a threshold where near-human robots provoke discomfort. Something about almost-but-not-quite human triggers rejection. Personalization has its own uncanny valley. There's a zone where communication is personalized enough to seem targeted but not personalized enough to feel genuine. This zone often provokes more negative response than no personalization at all. Consider receiving an email that opens with "I noticed your company recently expanded into the Midwest." If you did recently expand into the Midwest and the email goes on to say something relevant about that expansion, the personalization works. But if the email pivots immediately to generic content unrelated to geographic expansion, the personalization feels like a trick. You sense that someone researched one fact about you just to get your attention, not because they actually understand your situation.

Several patterns trigger uncanny valley responses. Surface-level personalization with generic substance uses someone's name, company, and one researched fact as window dressing for mass-produced content, and recipients recognize the pattern. Robotic personalization includes personalized elements but uses language patterns that sound like templates. "As a [job title] at [company name], you probably face [generic challenge]" reads as automation regardless of how accurate the bracketed content is. Excessive personalization references too many details about a prospect, which can feel intrusive rather than attentive. If you mention someone's college, their recent social media posts, their attendance at a specific event, and their company's quarterly earnings in a single email, you've crossed from informed to creepy. Inconsistent personalization begins with personalized content but shifts to generic language midway, signaling that personalization was bolted on rather than integrated.

Avoiding the uncanny valley requires genuine relevance throughout the communication, natural language that doesn't sound templated, appropriate restraint in how much personal information is referenced, and consistent quality across the entire message.

Segment-Level Versus Individual-Level Personalization

Not all personalization operates at the individual level. Segment-level personalization tailors content for groups who share characteristics rather than for specific individuals. Both approaches have legitimate applications. The choice depends on what the situation requires and what data supports. Individual-level personalization makes sense when you have meaningful data about specific individuals, when the audience is small enough to warrant individual attention, when deals are large enough to justify the effort, and when recipients expect individual treatment. Enterprise sales typically calls for individual personalization. Segment-level personalization makes sense when individual data is sparse, when the audience is large, when deals are smaller, and when the goal is reaching many people efficiently. Inside sales and marketing-led sales often operate at segment level.

Many organizations use hybrid approaches. Early outreach uses segment-level personalization. As prospects engage and reveal more about themselves, personalization shifts toward individual level. The journey begins with "relevant for people like you" and progresses toward "relevant for you specifically." AI enables both levels. For segment personalization, AI identifies meaningful segments, determines what content resonates with each segment, and automates delivery. For individual personalization, AI synthesizes available data about specific people and helps create tailored communication.

A commercial insurance company segments their prospects by industry and company size. Early outreach uses segment-tailored content: manufacturing companies receive manufacturing-relevant messaging, while hospitality companies receive hospitality-relevant content. When prospects engage, the system accumulates behavioral data. Eventually, enough information exists to personalize individually: this specific hospitality company cares most about liability coverage based on their downloads, while that one seems focused on property protection based on their questions. The transition from segment to individual happens naturally as data accumulates.

Personalization Across the Customer Lifecycle

Personalization shouldn't stop when deals close. Post-sale engagement benefits from the same tailored approach that wins new customers. Onboarding personalization adapts the customer introduction experience based on their specific needs and capabilities. A sophisticated technical buyer needs different onboarding than a first-time user. A customer who purchased for a specific use case needs onboarding focused on that use case. AI identifies customer types and tailors onboarding journeys accordingly. Usage-based communication responds to how customers actually use the product. A customer struggling with a feature receives help. A customer ignoring valuable functionality receives education about what they're missing. A customer using the product heavily receives recognition and possibly expansion conversations. AI monitors usage patterns and triggers appropriate engagement.

Renewal personalization tailors contract renewal discussions to each customer's situation. A customer with growing usage needs different conversation than one with flat usage. A customer who has expressed concerns needs different handling than one who has been satisfied. AI informs renewal strategy with customer-specific intelligence. Cross-sell and upsell personalization recommends additional products and services based on what each customer is likely to need. Timing matters as much as relevance. AI identifies when customers reach points where additional offerings make sense and suggests what to recommend. This lifecycle personalization increases customer value by driving adoption, reducing churn, and expanding revenue. It also improves customer experience by making interactions feel relevant rather than random.

Implementing Personalization at Scale

Moving from sporadic personalization to systematic personalization at scale requires more than tools. It requires process redesign. Start with the data foundation. Personalization depends on knowing things about recipients, so before implementing personalization technology, assess what data you have, what additional data you need, and how data flows between systems. Gaps in data produce gaps in personalization. Build your content assets as well. AI can assemble and customize content, but it needs raw material to work with. Develop libraries of content components that can be mixed and matched: value propositions by segment, proof points by industry, messaging variations by persona. The richness of these libraries determines the quality of personalized output.

Focus on workflow integration because personalization tools that exist outside the normal workflow won't get used consistently. Integrate AI personalization into the platforms salespeople already use. The capability should feel like a natural part of working, not an additional step. Establish quality control by creating review processes that catch personalization failures before they reach recipients. This might mean human review of all AI-generated content, sampling-based review, or exception-based review that flags content meeting certain criteria for human attention.

Commit to measurement by tracking whether personalization is actually improving results. Compare response rates, conversion rates, and deal values from personalized engagement versus alternatives. If personalization isn't measurably better, something needs adjustment. Finally, embrace iteration. Personalization quality improves over time as systems learn what works and content libraries expand. Build feedback loops that capture what resonates and what doesn't. Treat personalization as a capability to be developed continuously, not a project to be completed.

The Efficiency Question

The previous chapter examined how AI helps salespeople understand customers. This chapter examined how AI helps translate that understanding into personalized engagement. Both capabilities improve sales effectiveness. But effectiveness isn't the only concern. Efficiency matters too. Salespeople have limited time. Every hour spent on one activity is unavailable for another. Even the most effective practices create value only if they fit within the constraints of available time. The next chapter turns to efficiency directly. AI doesn't just help salespeople do better work. It helps them do more work by eliminating time drains, automating administrative burden, and freeing hours for activities that require human attention. Understanding where AI can recover time, and where human time remains essential, shapes how salespeople allocate their most scarce resource.

Chapter Six

The Efficiency Edge

Where the Time Goes

Ask salespeople what limits their performance, and the answer is rarely skill or motivation. It's time. There isn't enough of it. Between research, prospecting, meetings, follow-ups, proposals, administrative tasks, and internal demands, the day fills completely before high-value activities get proper attention.

Research consistently shows that salespeople spend less than a third of their working hours actually selling. The rest disappears into activities that support selling but don't directly generate revenue: updating CRM records, preparing for meetings, writing emails, attending internal calls, and handling administrative requirements. This isn't unique to struggling performers. Even top salespeople face the same time pressure. They've just found ways to manage it more effectively.

AI transforms this time equation. It doesn't add hours to the day. It recovers hours that currently go to tasks machines can handle. Every hour reclaimed is available for customer conversations, relationship building, and the creative work of closing deals. The efficiency gains aren't incremental. They're substantial enough to change what a salesperson can accomplish. Understanding where AI can recover time, and where human time remains necessary, determines whether you use these capabilities effectively or waste them on the wrong problems.

The Administrative Burden

Administrative tasks consume a staggering portion of sales time. CRM updates, expense reports, activity logging, contact data maintenance, meeting scheduling, and documentation requirements pile up throughout every day. None of these activities generates revenue directly. All of them feel like obstacles to actual selling. The frustration isn't irrational. Administrative burden has real costs. When salespeople spend thirty minutes daily updating CRM records, that's two and a half hours weekly, ten hours monthly, and one hundred twenty hours annually. A single administrative task that seems minor multiplied across a year becomes a meaningful chunk of productive capacity.

Organizations impose these requirements for legitimate reasons. Accurate CRM data enables forecasting, coaching, and strategic decisions. Documentation protects against relationship loss when people leave. Activity tracking provides visibility into what's working. The problem isn't that administration is unnecessary. The problem is that humans are doing work machines could handle. AI automation addresses administrative burden at multiple levels. Automatic data capture records interactions without manual entry. Smart scheduling handles meeting coordination. Template generation produces routine documents. Workflow automation routes tasks and notifications. Each automation eliminates time that was previously lost to administrative friction.

The compound effect matters more than any individual automation. If AI saves ten minutes on CRM updates, fifteen minutes on scheduling, twenty minutes on email drafting, and another twenty minutes across various small tasks, that's over an hour daily. An hour daily is five hours weekly. Five hours weekly is significant capacity for customer engagement.

Automated Data Capture

CRM systems are only useful when they contain accurate, current data. Salespeople know this. They also know that entering data takes time they don't have. The result is a predictable pattern: CRM records are incomplete, outdated, or both. The system that's supposed to enable better selling instead reflects a fragmented picture of reality. AI-powered data capture changes this dynamic by recording information automatically from interactions that happen naturally.

Email integration captures contact information, conversation content, and relationship signals from email exchanges. When a salesperson emails a prospect, the system logs the interaction, extracts relevant data, and updates records without manual entry. New contacts get created automatically. Existing records get refreshed. Activity history accumulates without effort. Calendar integration records meetings, attendees, and associated accounts, knowing who met with whom, when, and for how long. Meeting patterns become visible: which accounts are getting attention, which are being neglected, and how time allocation matches priority.

Call recording integration logs phone interactions and, with conversation intelligence tools, extracts key information from what was discussed. The CRM record includes not just that a call happened but what topics were covered, what commitments were made, and what follow-up is needed. Social integration tracks relevant interactions on professional networks, flowing information into the CRM automatically when contacts engage with company content, change roles, or share relevant updates. The cumulative effect is CRM data that stays current without consuming salesperson time. Records reflect actual relationship activity rather than whatever salespeople remembered to enter. Data quality improves while administrative burden decreases.

Natalie manages a team selling marketing services. Before implementing automated data capture, her CRM contained records that were months out of date. Contacts had changed jobs without updates. Conversations had happened without logging. Pipeline stages didn't reflect current reality. After implementation, records update continuously. She can trust what the system shows. Her salespeople spend the time they used to spend on data entry on actual selling instead.

Meeting Preparation and Summarization

Meetings dominate sales work. Discovery calls, presentations, negotiations, and check-ins fill calendars. Each meeting requires preparation beforehand and follow-up afterward. Both activities take time that could go elsewhere.

AI assists on both ends. Pre-meeting preparation traditionally requires researching the prospect, reviewing past interactions, checking recent news, and planning discussion topics. A thorough preparation might take thirty minutes or more. AI compresses this time by generating briefings automatically. Before a meeting, the salesperson receives a summary: who will be there, their roles and backgrounds, key points from previous conversations, recent company developments, and suggested topics. The briefing synthesizes information that would have taken significant time to assemble manually.

Post-meeting summarization captures what happened and what comes next. Traditional approaches require salespeople to write notes after each call. AI-powered conversation intelligence generates summaries automatically from recorded meetings. Key topics get identified. Action items get extracted. Relevant moments get flagged for review. The salesperson reviews and refines the summary rather than creating it from scratch.

The time savings compound across many meetings. A salesperson with eight meetings daily who saves twenty minutes of preparation and ten minutes of summarization per meeting recovers four hours. That's half the workday available for activities that AI can't handle. Beyond time savings, AI assistance improves preparation and summarization quality. Human-generated notes are selective and sometimes inaccurate. AI captures comprehensively. Human preparation often misses relevant information buried in past interactions. AI surfaces it systematically. The work isn't just faster. It's better.

Email Efficiency

Email consumes enormous sales time. Writing messages, responding to inquiries, following up with prospects, and managing inbox volume fill hours that could go to higher-value activities. The average salesperson sends and receives dozens of emails daily. Each one takes time to compose, review, and send.

AI email assistance works at several levels. Draft generation produces initial email content based on context. The salesperson specifies the intent: follow up on last week's demo, respond to this objection, request a meeting with this stakeholder. AI generates a draft that addresses the intent with appropriate content. The salesperson edits rather than writes from scratch. Response suggestions propose replies to incoming messages. When an email arrives, AI analyzes the content and generates potential responses. The salesperson selects, modifies, or rejects suggestions. For routine messages, this reduces response time significantly.

Template personalization adapts standard templates for specific recipients. Rather than using identical language for every prospect, AI customizes templates based on recipient characteristics and history. The message retains template efficiency while gaining personalization effectiveness. Inbox prioritization identifies which messages need attention first by analyzing incoming email for urgency, sender importance, and content relevance. It surfaces what matters and pushes down what doesn't. Salespeople focus on messages that warrant attention rather than processing everything in arrival order. Follow-up reminders track conversations that need responses and alert salespeople when messages go unanswered. Rather than mentally tracking dozens of pending threads, salespeople receive prompts when follow-up is needed.

The efficiency gains from email assistance are substantial because email volume is so high. Saving two minutes per email across fifty daily emails means one hundred minutes recovered. Multiply by working days, and email efficiency becomes one of the highest-return AI applications available.

Scheduling Automation

Meeting scheduling seems like a minor task. One scheduling interaction takes just minutes. But those minutes multiply across countless requests throughout every week. The back-and-forth of finding mutually available times, sending calendar invites, handling reschedules, and coordinating across time zones adds up to significant lost time. AI scheduling assistants handle this coordination automatically. The salesperson indicates they want to meet with someone. The assistant accesses calendar availability, proposes times to the other party, handles the response, sends confirmations, and creates the calendar event. The salesperson's involvement drops from multiple exchanges to a single request.

Scheduling automation works particularly well for external meetings where traditional back-and-forth is common. Instead of exchanging multiple emails to find a time, the assistant handles negotiation automatically. Many prospects actually prefer this efficiency to the traditional process. Internal meeting coordination benefits as well. Gathering multiple participants for an internal call requires checking several calendars and finding alignment. AI assistants identify available slots across all required attendees and propose options. What previously required several messages happens in one step. The efficiency extends to scheduling logistics beyond timing. Room booking, video conference link generation, agenda distribution, and pre-meeting materials can all integrate with scheduling automation. The meeting gets set up completely rather than requiring separate steps for each element.

Victor sells enterprise technology and typically has fifteen to twenty external meetings weekly. Before implementing scheduling automation, coordinating these meetings consumed about five hours of his week. His assistant now handles the coordination. Those five hours go to customer conversations and deal strategy instead. His calendar stays full, but scheduling no longer competes with selling for his attention.

Document Generation

Sales involves continuous document creation. Proposals, contracts, presentations, quotes, and follow-up summaries all require production. Each document takes time to create, and customization takes additional time beyond starting from templates.

AI document generation accelerates this work in several ways. Proposal automation produces customized proposals based on deal parameters and prospect characteristics. The system knows what the prospect needs, what pricing applies, what terms are standard, and what customizations are required. It generates a draft proposal that addresses the specific opportunity. The salesperson reviews and refines rather than building from components manually. Contract generation creates agreements based on negotiated terms. When deal parameters are established, AI produces contract drafts that incorporate the specific provisions. Legal review still applies, but initial drafting happens automatically.

Presentation customization adapts slide decks for specific audiences. Rather than manually modifying master presentations for each meeting, AI adjusts content, examples, and emphasis based on the audience. A presentation for a technical buyer emphasizes different elements than one for an executive buyer. Quote generation calculates and formats pricing for specific configurations. Complex products with multiple options and pricing structures require careful quote assembly. AI handles the configuration and produces professional quotes ready for customer delivery. Follow-up document creation produces meeting summaries, action item lists, and next-step documents. After important conversations, these documents reinforce what was discussed and clarify the path forward. AI generates drafts from conversation records, saving time while improving consistency.

Document generation efficiency compounds across the sales cycle. A deal might require multiple proposal versions, several presentations, a series of quotes, and contract drafts before closing. AI assistance on each document adds up to substantial time savings per opportunity.

Research Automation

Sales research takes time. Understanding a prospect's business, industry, competitive situation, and relevant news requires gathering information from multiple sources. Thorough research improves conversation quality but competes with other demands for limited time. AI research automation handles information gathering and synthesis. Instead of salespeople visiting multiple websites, reading through articles, and assembling notes, AI collects and organizes relevant information automatically.

Company research pulls together information about prospect organizations: what they do, how they're structured, recent developments, financial situation, and strategic direction. AI synthesizes this from public sources into digestible briefings. Contact research gathers background on specific people: their role, career history, public statements, and social presence. Understanding who you're meeting provides context for more effective conversations. Industry research identifies trends, challenges, and developments relevant to the prospect's sector. Industry context helps salespeople speak credibly about the environment their prospects operate in.

Competitive intelligence tracks what competitors are doing: their messaging, their wins and losses, their product announcements, and their market positioning. AI monitors competitor activity and surfaces relevant information when it matters. News monitoring watches for developments that create sales opportunities or affect existing deals. A prospect company announcing expansion, leadership changes, or strategic initiatives represents relevant intelligence. AI surfaces these developments automatically rather than requiring manual monitoring.

The research efficiency gain isn't just time saved. It's research actually happening. Without AI assistance, time pressure often means research gets skipped or done superficially. With AI assistance, comprehensive research becomes feasible for every opportunity.

Workflow Automation

Beyond individual task efficiency, AI automates entire workflows that previously required manual coordination. Lead routing automatically directs new leads to appropriate salespeople based on territory, expertise, capacity, and other factors. Leads flow to the right person without manual assignment. Task sequencing schedules follow-up activities based on deal stages and engagement patterns. When a prospect takes a specific action, the system creates appropriate tasks and reminders for the salesperson. Approval workflows route deals requiring special authorization through appropriate channels. Discounts beyond threshold, non-standard terms, or large deals flow to approvers automatically with relevant context.

Handoff coordination manages transitions between sales stages or team members. When opportunities move from one phase to another, relevant information transfers and appropriate people get notified. Alert generation notifies salespeople when important events occur. A key contact views the proposal. A competitor mention occurs in a monitored publication. Usage patterns shift at an existing account. Alerts surface what matters without requiring constant monitoring. These workflow automations eliminate coordination overhead that accumulates across many small interactions. Each individual routing decision or approval request seems minor. Collectively, workflow friction consumes significant time and creates delays that affect customer experience.

The Reinvestment Question

Efficiency gains from AI create recovered time. The question becomes what to do with that time. The answer matters as much as the efficiency gains themselves. The default often disappoints. Salespeople gain time from automation, then find that time absorbed by other low-value activities. Internal meetings expand. Administrative requirements creep back. The efficiency evaporates without producing results.

Intentional reinvestment prevents this outcome. Organizations and individuals should decide in advance how recovered time will be used. More customer contact is the obvious reinvestment. If AI recovers an hour daily from administrative work, that hour could go to additional prospecting calls, more thorough discovery conversations, or deeper relationship maintenance with existing accounts. Higher-quality preparation uses efficiency gains for depth rather than volume. Instead of more meetings, the same number of meetings with better preparation. Instead of more proposals, better-customized proposals with more strategic thinking behind them.

Skill development invests recovered time in building capabilities. Learning new approaches, developing industry expertise, or improving specific selling skills. This investment compounds over time. Strategic thinking uses efficiency gains for work that typically gets crowded out. Account planning, competitive strategy, or territory optimization. These activities improve results but rarely feel urgent enough to prioritize in time-constrained days. Personal sustainability acknowledges that salespeople are human. Some efficiency gains might reasonably go to better work-life balance rather than more work. Sustainable performance matters more than maximum short-term output. The choice depends on individual circumstances and organizational priorities. What matters is making the choice deliberately rather than letting recovered time dissipate into whatever activities expand to fill it.

Measuring Efficiency Impact

Efficiency gains deserve measurement. Intuition about time savings often proves inaccurate. Actual measurement reveals what's working and what isn't. Time tracking quantifies how time gets spent before and after AI implementation. This doesn't require elaborate systems. Simple sampling or periodic logging provides data on time allocation across activities. Changes after AI adoption become visible. Activity metrics track volume of productive activities. Number of calls made, meetings held, proposals sent, and opportunities advanced. If efficiency gains are being reinvested in customer engagement, these metrics should improve.

Output ratios compare results to time invested. Revenue per hour worked. Deals closed per month. Pipeline generated per week. These ratios capture whether efficiency is translating to productivity. Capacity indicators assess whether salespeople have room for additional opportunities. If efficiency gains are real but salespeople still feel overwhelmed, something is wrong with reinvestment or measurement. Quality metrics ensure efficiency isn't undermining effectiveness. Response times, customer satisfaction, and deal quality should maintain or improve as efficiency increases. If they're declining, automation may be cutting corners that shouldn't be cut. Measurement creates accountability for efficiency investments. Tools that promise time savings should deliver measurable improvement. If they don't, reconsider the tool or the implementation.

The Limit of Efficiency

Efficiency matters, but it isn't everything. At some point, doing things faster stops being the constraint. Doing the right things becomes more important. The most efficient approach to a bad strategy produces bad results faster. Automating the wrong activities saves time on work that shouldn't happen at all. Optimizing processes that don't serve customers creates no real value.

This observation sets up an important distinction. Efficiency addresses how you work. Effectiveness addresses what you work on and how well you do it. AI contributes to both, but the contributions are different. Efficiency improvements are largely technical. Better tools, smoother processes, and faster execution. These improvements can often be implemented systematically across an organization.

Effectiveness improvements require judgment. Which opportunities deserve attention? How should complex situations be handled? What trade-offs should be made when interests conflict? These questions don't have technical answers. They require human capability that AI can inform but not replace. The most successful salespeople combine efficiency and effectiveness. They use AI to handle tasks machines do well, then invest the recovered time in high-judgment activities where human capability matters most. They don't just work faster. They work smarter about where to apply their uniquely human strengths.

Understanding what those strengths are, and what AI fundamentally cannot do regardless of efficiency gains, is essential for making good decisions about how to allocate effort. The next chapter examines the boundaries of AI capability and identifies the irreplaceable human elements that will continue to distinguish successful sales professionals.

Chapter Seven

What AI Can't Do

The Boundary That Matters

The previous chapters examined what AI can do for sales. This chapter examines what it can't. Understanding this boundary isn't pessimism about technology. It's clarity about where human effort creates irreplaceable value. Every tool has limits. Understanding those limits determines whether you use the tool well or misapply it. A hammer drives nails effectively. It doesn't help with screws. A salesperson who knows this reaches for the right tool at the right time. A salesperson who doesn't wastes effort and damages outcomes.

AI limits aren't temporary gaps that better technology will soon fill. Some are fundamental constraints that stem from what AI is and how it works. Others reflect the nature of human relationships that define complex selling. Both categories matter for understanding where to invest human attention. The salespeople who thrive with AI won't be those who expect it to do everything. They'll be those who recognize the boundary clearly and focus their energy on the human side of that boundary. This chapter maps that territory.

Trust Is Human

Trust sits at the center of complex sales. Customers don't buy expensive solutions from companies they don't trust. They don't share sensitive information with salespeople they don't trust. They don't take career risks on recommendations from sources they don't trust. The entire architecture of enterprise selling rests on a foundation of trust that must be built before transactions can occur.

AI doesn't build trust. It processes information, identifies patterns, and generates outputs. It doesn't have character that customers can assess. It doesn't demonstrate reliability over time through consistent behavior. It doesn't put skin in the game by making commitments and keeping them. It doesn't show vulnerability or admit uncertainty in ways that create human connection. Trust develops through repeated interaction where someone's character is tested and proven. A customer learns to trust a salesperson by watching how they handle difficult situations. Do they tell hard truths or just what the customer wants to hear? Do they recommend what's best for the customer or what's best for their commission? Do they follow through on commitments or find excuses when things get difficult?

These character tests can only be passed by humans. AI can assist by ensuring salespeople have information they need to follow through. AI can help salespeople remember commitments they made. But the character being evaluated is human character. The trust being built is trust in a person. Consider what happens when a major deal goes wrong. Implementation struggles. Results fall short of expectations. The customer is frustrated. This moment tests the relationship. A trusted salesperson who shows up, takes responsibility, and works to fix problems can actually strengthen the relationship through the difficulty. An untrusted salesperson facing the same situation loses the account. AI has no role to play in the character that shows up in that moment.

Reading the Room

Sales conversations contain multiple layers of communication. Words carry explicit meaning. Tone, timing, body language, and context carry implicit meaning. Often, what customers don't say matters more than what they do say. Reading these layers requires human perception that AI doesn't possess. A customer says "we need to think about it" after a presentation. The words are neutral. The meaning depends on everything surrounding them. Were they leaning forward with interest or sitting back with arms crossed? Did they ask clarifying questions that suggest engagement or stay silent? Did their tone suggest genuine deliberation or polite rejection? Did the pause before speaking indicate careful thought or discomfort with delivering bad news?

Experienced salespeople process these signals automatically. They know when "we need to think about it" means genuine consideration and when it means they've lost. They adjust their approach based on what they're reading. They probe differently when they sense resistance than when they sense hesitation about process. AI can analyze recorded conversations after the fact. It can track sentiment indicators and identify patterns across many calls. But it can't read the room in real time the way humans can. It can't catch the micro-expression that crosses a stakeholder's face when a competitor is mentioned. It can't feel the energy shift when budget comes up. It can't sense the political dynamics playing out beneath the surface of formal discussion. This real-time reading matters because sales conversations aren't scripted. What you say next should depend on what just happened. The question you ask, the example you share, the concern you address all need to respond to the moment. AI can prepare you for conversations. It can't navigate them for you.

Creative Problem-Solving

Standardized solutions work for standardized problems. Complex sales involve non-standard situations that require creative problem-solving. A customer has constraints that don't fit your normal approach. A deal has political dynamics that require unusual structure. A negotiation reaches impasse that standard tactics won't resolve. These situations demand creativity that AI doesn't possess.

AI generates outputs based on patterns from training data. When situations resemble what it has seen before, it performs well. When situations diverge from previous patterns, it struggles. Novel problems that require genuinely new solutions fall outside its capabilities. Sales creativity takes many forms. It might mean finding a pricing structure that works for a customer's unusual budget cycle. It might mean identifying a use case the product wasn't designed for but can actually serve. It might mean structuring a pilot program that reduces risk enough for a hesitant buyer to proceed. It might mean connecting people across organizations in ways that create new possibilities.

Consider a salesperson whose champion leaves the target organization mid-deal. This scenario has infinite variations depending on why they left, who replaced them, what relationships existed with other stakeholders, and how far the deal had progressed. There's no formula to follow. The salesperson must assess the new situation, identify creative options, and execute a recovery strategy that fits the specific circumstances. AI can provide information that informs this process. It can't generate the creative solution. Human creativity also applies to relationship building in ways AI can't replicate. Finding the shared interest that creates personal connection. Identifying the mutual acquaintance who can provide introduction. Recognizing the opportunity to add value in unexpected ways. These creative acts strengthen relationships beyond transactional exchange.

Judgment Under Uncertainty

Sales involves continuous decisions under uncertainty. Should I pursue this opportunity or focus elsewhere? Should I push for a meeting or wait for them to come to me? Should I introduce additional stakeholders or keep the conversation focused? Should I discount to win or hold price and risk losing? Each decision involves incomplete information and uncertain outcomes. AI can provide data that informs these decisions. It can offer predictions based on historical patterns. But it can't make the judgment calls that combine data with context, values, and wisdom. Those calls require human judgment.

The limitation isn't information processing. AI processes more information than humans. The limitation is that judgment involves weighing factors that can't be fully quantified. How much does this customer's satisfaction matter for future referrals? How will aggressive pricing affect market perception? What's the right balance between closing quickly and closing at optimal terms? These questions have no objectively correct answers. They require judgment that reflects priorities, values, and strategic thinking. Judgment also involves accountability that AI can't bear. When a salesperson makes a call, they own the consequences. They can explain their reasoning, learn from outcomes, and adjust future decisions. AI recommendations carry no such accountability. They're inputs to human decisions, not substitutes for them.

Amanda sells consulting services to financial institutions. Every engagement requires estimating scope under uncertainty. The client's problems are partially hidden. The solutions will evolve as work progresses. She must judge whether her team can deliver what she's proposing and whether the pricing will prove sustainable. These judgments draw on experience, intuition, and understanding of her firm's capabilities that no AI system possesses. Her track record of sound judgment is why clients trust her to scope work that will succeed.

Emotional Intelligence

Sales is emotional work. Customers feel anxiety about making wrong decisions. They feel excitement about possibilities. They feel frustration when things don't work as expected. They feel loyalty to relationships that have served them well. These emotions influence decisions as much as rational analysis does. Emotional intelligence enables salespeople to recognize emotions, respond appropriately, and manage emotional dynamics of sales relationships. It's what allows a salesperson to sense when a customer is overwhelmed and needs reassurance. It's what enables reading unspoken concerns and addressing them before they become objections. It's what makes the difference between a conversation that feels transactional and one that feels genuinely supportive.

AI can detect some emotional signals through sentiment analysis. It can identify that a customer's language patterns suggest frustration or that their tone indicates uncertainty. But detection isn't the same as response. Knowing that someone is anxious doesn't tell you how to help them feel more confident. That requires empathy, which is the ability to understand another person's emotional state and respond in ways that serve them. Emotional intelligence also involves managing your own emotions in service of the relationship. Staying calm when a customer is angry. Remaining patient when a deal stalls. Sustaining optimism through rejection. Channeling competitive drive without becoming desperate. These emotional regulation skills can't be outsourced to AI. They're internal capacities that salespeople must develop and maintain. The emotional dimension matters especially in difficult moments. A customer calls furious about a problem. The salesperson's emotional response in that moment shapes whether the relationship survives. Defensiveness escalates conflict. Genuine empathy and ownership begins repair. This isn't about technique. It's about actual emotional capacity that shows up under pressure.

Ethical Reasoning

Sales situations regularly involve ethical dimensions. Should I disclose this limitation of our product even though the customer hasn't asked? Should I pursue this deal knowing the customer might not be a good fit? Should I use information I obtained in confidence to advance my position? Should I pressure a hesitant buyer when I'm not sure the solution is right for them? These questions require ethical reasoning that AI can't provide. AI doesn't have values. It doesn't experience the moral weight of decisions. It can't judge whether an action is right or wrong in the full sense those words carry. It processes inputs and generates outputs. Moral reasoning requires something more.

Ethical selling matters beyond philosophy. Customers sense integrity. They can tell when salespeople operate from genuine concern for customer welfare versus pure self-interest. This sensing influences trust, which influences deals. Short-term ethical shortcuts often produce long-term relationship damage. AI actually increases the importance of ethical reasoning by expanding what salespeople can do. With more information about customers, more ability to personalize at scale, and more tools for influence, the opportunities for manipulation grow alongside the opportunities for service. The technology is neutral. Whether it's used ethically depends entirely on human choices. Strong salespeople develop ethical frameworks that guide their decisions. They know what lines they won't cross regardless of pressure. They make choices based on principles rather than momentary advantage. This ethical foundation can't be programmed into AI. It must be cultivated in people.

Long-Term Relationship Investment

Some relationship investments pay off only over extended time horizons. A salesperson stays in touch with a contact who can't buy now but might in the future. A vendor supports a customer through a difficult period without expecting immediate return. A trusted advisor gives guidance that doesn't advance any deal but strengthens the relationship. AI doesn't make these long-term investments because AI doesn't have genuine long-term interest in relationships. It processes current inputs and generates current outputs. It doesn't care about relationships. It doesn't think about next year or the year after. The patience and persistence that characterize strong sales relationships are human qualities.

This long-term orientation matters because complex sales involve extended cycles and ongoing relationships. The customer you help today may buy in two years. The contact who can't help you now may become your biggest champion later. The relationship you maintain through their job change may open doors at their new company. Human salespeople can choose to invest in relationships beyond what short-term returns justify. They can maintain connections because the connections matter, not just because they calculate expected value. This authenticity shows up in relationships. Customers know the difference between salespeople who care about them and salespeople who just care about deals.

The Human Skills Premium

The existence of AI capabilities increases the value of capabilities AI lacks. When machines handle research, data entry, and routine communication, what remains is the work that requires human capability. That work becomes the basis for differentiation. This dynamic mirrors what happened in other fields. When computers automated calculation, the value of pure arithmetic skill declined while the value of mathematical reasoning increased. When design software automated layout, the value of technical execution declined while the value of creative vision increased. When translation tools automated basic language conversion, the value of literal translation declined while the value of cultural nuance and contextual judgment increased.

In sales, AI automation shifts value toward human capabilities that can't be automated. The salesperson whose only contribution was information retrieval and basic communication loses relevance. The salesperson who builds deep trust, reads complex situations, exercises sound judgment, and provides genuine counsel becomes more valuable because those capabilities remain scarce while routine capabilities become abundant. This isn't a temporary phenomenon. It reflects the fundamental division between what machines do well and what humans do well. Machine capabilities will continue advancing, but they'll advance in machine-appropriate directions. Human capabilities will remain the province of humans. The implication for career development is clear. Invest in capabilities that AI won't replicate. Trust-building, emotional intelligence, creative problem-solving, ethical reasoning, and judgment under uncertainty deserve priority. These aren't soft skills in the sense of being less important. They're the core competencies that will define successful sales professionals in an AI-augmented world.

Working With AI, Not Like AI

Understanding what AI can't do clarifies how to work with it effectively. The goal isn't to become more machine-like. It's to become more distinctly human in a partnership with machine capabilities. This means using AI for what it does well: processing information, identifying patterns, handling routine tasks, and providing data that informs decisions. It means preserving human energy for what humans do well: building relationships, navigating ambiguity, making judgment calls, and bringing genuine emotional presence to interactions. The partnership works when each partner contributes their strengths. It fails when humans try to do machine work or when machines are expected to do human work. Clarity about the boundary enables effective collaboration.

Consider a typical sales day with good AI partnership. AI surfaces the accounts that need attention based on behavioral signals. The salesperson reviews the list and adds judgment about which accounts to prioritize based on strategic factors AI doesn't weigh. AI provides briefings for upcoming meetings. The salesperson reviews them and adds personal knowledge that isn't in systems. AI transcribes and summarizes calls. The salesperson reflects on what happened emotionally and relationally beyond what transcripts capture. AI drafts follow-up communications. The salesperson adds authentic voice and genuine personalization. Throughout, human and machine contributions are complementary. Neither tries to do the other's job. The salesperson isn't fighting the technology or feeling threatened by it. They're leveraging it while investing their distinctly human capabilities where they matter most.

Developing Human Capability

The human skills that AI can't replicate deserve intentional development. They don't improve automatically through experience. They require deliberate practice and reflection.

Trust-building develops through consistent follow-through over time. Commit to what you can deliver. Deliver what you commit. Tell hard truths rather than comfortable lies. Demonstrate that customer interests guide your recommendations. Trust builds through accumulated evidence of trustworthy behavior.

Reading the room improves through attention and feedback. After conversations, reflect on what you noticed and what you missed. Ask colleagues to share what they observed that you didn't. Study how skilled negotiators and communicators read situations. Practice noticing more and reacting to what you notice.

Creative problem-solving expands through exposure to diverse situations and solutions. Study how others have handled unusual problems. Build a repertoire of approaches that can be adapted. When facing novel situations, generate multiple options before selecting one. Practice flexible thinking that questions assumptions.

Judgment matures through making decisions, observing outcomes, and reflecting honestly on results. Keep records of important calls and what happened. Look for patterns in what you got right and wrong. Seek feedback from people whose judgment you respect. Accept that judgment develops slowly through accumulated experience.

Emotional intelligence grows through self-awareness and practice. Notice your emotional reactions and their effects on your behavior. Observe how others respond to different emotional approaches. Practice staying present with difficult emotions rather than avoiding them. Develop capacity to manage your state while remaining authentic.

These development paths don't offer quick fixes. The capabilities are deep and take years to develop fully. But they're also the capabilities that will distinguish successful salespeople for as long as sales requires human relationships.

The Partnership Model

The relationship between human salespeople and AI tools resembles a partnership more than a hierarchy. Neither party is simply boss or servant. Each contributes different capabilities to shared objectives. Effective partnerships require mutual understanding. Each partner needs to know what the other can contribute and where they need support. The mapping provided in this chapter and the preceding ones offers that understanding. AI contributes information processing, pattern recognition, efficiency, and scale. Humans contribute trust, emotional intelligence, judgment, creativity, and ethical reasoning. With this understanding, salespeople can approach AI as capable partners rather than either threats to resist or magic solutions to adopt uncritically. The partnership produces results neither could achieve alone. That's what makes it valuable.

But partnerships also require managing how others perceive them. Customers have their own views about AI in sales relationships. Some welcome the efficiency and capability AI enables. Others feel uncomfortable with automation in what they want to be human relationships. Understanding and managing these customer perceptions becomes its own skill. The next chapter examines how AI affects trust dynamics with customers. As AI becomes more visible in sales interactions, the relationship between automation and authenticity becomes something salespeople must navigate actively. Earning and maintaining trust in an increasingly automated world presents both challenges and opportunities.

Chapter Eight

Earning Trust in an Automated World

The Trust Question

Customers increasingly know that AI is involved in sales interactions. They receive emails that might be AI-drafted. They interact with chatbots that might be AI-powered. They encounter personalization that might be AI-generated. This awareness creates questions about authenticity that didn't exist when sales was purely human work. The questions are reasonable. Is this salesperson actually paying attention to me, or is a machine doing the work? Does the personalization reflect genuine understanding, or just data manipulation? Is this relationship real, or am I interacting with an algorithm wearing a human face?

How salespeople handle these questions affects whether AI helps or hurts their customer relationships. Handled poorly, AI integration erodes the trust that complex sales require. Handled well, it can actually strengthen trust by demonstrating competence and delivering better service. The difference lies in how salespeople approach transparency, authenticity, and the positioning of AI in their customer interactions. This chapter examines how to build and maintain trust when AI is part of your sales toolkit. The principles aren't complicated, but applying them consistently requires intentional effort.

The Transparency Spectrum

Transparency about AI use ranges from full disclosure to complete concealment. Neither extreme serves well. The right approach sits somewhere in the middle, varying by context and customer expectation. Full disclosure of every AI touchpoint would be absurd. Nobody expects salespeople to announce "this email was drafted with AI assistance" or "my scheduling assistant is actually software." These uses are unremarkable and mentioning them would seem strange. The AI is simply a tool, no different from the word processor used to format a proposal or the phone used to make a call.

Complete concealment creates different problems. When customers feel deceived about AI involvement, trust suffers severely. If a customer believes they're receiving personalized human attention but discovers they're actually interacting with automation, the betrayal damages the relationship beyond whatever value the automation provided. The middle ground involves transparency about AI use when it matters to the customer's understanding of the relationship. This means being straightforward when asked, when concealment would create false impressions, or when disclosure would actually increase customer confidence. It means not announcing AI involvement when it's irrelevant but not hiding it when it's significant. Context determines what counts as significant. A customer who values being known by their salesperson would reasonably want to know if AI is generating the "personal" touches they appreciate. A customer who cares primarily about results wouldn't need to know the tools used to achieve them. Reading these contextual differences is part of the relationship management that good salespeople perform.

When Disclosure Helps

Some situations call for proactive disclosure because transparency actually strengthens the relationship.

When AI demonstrates investment. A salesperson using AI to research a prospect's company thoroughly can mention the research as evidence of preparation. Saying "I used our intelligence tools to understand your recent expansion initiatives" shows effort and capability. The customer learns that the salesperson came prepared through a combination of human attention and technological assistance. Both matter.

When AI enables better service. If AI tools allow faster response, more comprehensive analysis, or better follow-through, explaining this can increase customer confidence. Customers want to know they're working with a well-equipped partner. A salesperson who says "we track a lot of signals across your industry to stay current" positions AI capability as customer benefit rather than something to hide.

When customers are curious. Some customers, particularly in technical industries, are interested in what tools their vendors use. They appreciate sophisticated approaches and may even want to learn from them. For these customers, discussing AI capabilities openly creates connection rather than distance.

When disclosure preempts concern. If a customer might eventually realize AI is involved and feel deceived, proactive disclosure prevents that problem. Better to explain "our follow-up system helps me track all my commitments to customers" than to have a customer wonder why every email arrives at precisely the same time.

The common thread is disclosure positioned as benefit rather than confession. The salesperson isn't apologizing for using AI. They're showing that they're equipped with tools that help them serve customers better.

When Concealment Backfires

Certain concealment patterns reliably damage trust when discovered.

Passing AI work off as personal effort. If a salesperson implies they personally researched something that AI actually compiled, or personally wrote something that AI drafted, discovery of this misrepresentation undermines everything else in the relationship. Customers wonder what else might not be as it appeared.

Faking personal attention. Communication designed to seem individually crafted when it's actually mass-produced creates similar risk. The customer who receives a "personal" note and later realizes it went to hundreds of people feels foolish for having valued it. The relationship is damaged because the customer now questions what's genuine.

Hiding bot interactions. When customers interact with chatbots or AI assistants but believe they're communicating with humans, eventual discovery causes resentment. The deception is often unnecessary because many customers actually prefer the instant availability that automated channels provide.

Denying AI use when asked. If a customer directly asks whether AI was involved in something and the salesperson lies, trust destruction is severe and deserved. Direct questions deserve honest answers regardless of how the salesperson thinks the customer might react.

The pattern across these scenarios is deception about things that matter to the customer's understanding of the relationship. The remedy isn't compulsive disclosure. It's avoiding active misrepresentation about how attention is being paid and work is being done.

Authenticity in AI-Assisted Communication

AI can draft messages, but customers want to connect with humans. This creates tension that must be managed through how AI assistance is actually used. The problem isn't AI involvement. The problem is communication that feels artificial regardless of how it was produced. Customers can sense when messaging lacks genuine human voice. Whether AI generated it or a human wrote formulaic copy, inauthenticity registers. The solution involves ensuring AI assistance produces genuinely personal communication rather than just technically personalized communication. Several practices help.

Edit for voice. AI drafts should be starting points, not final products. The salesperson's editing should add genuine voice that reflects their actual personality and perspective. This isn't just changing a few words. It's ensuring the message would sound natural if read aloud by the salesperson who's sending it.

Add personal observation. Beyond whatever data-driven personalization AI provides, include something genuinely personal. A comment on recent news the salesperson actually found interesting. A connection to something from a previous conversation. A perspective the salesperson actually holds. These elements can't be generated. They must be added.

Respond to context. AI drafts are generated from data available at drafting time. They can't account for context the salesperson knows: a recent conversation with a colleague who knows the prospect, a sense that something is off based on interaction patterns, an intuition that the usual approach won't work this time. Human response to context distinguishes authentic communication from mechanical messaging.

Maintain consistency. A salesperson whose communication style varies wildly between interactions creates confusion. If AI-assisted messages sound different from direct conversation, customers notice the inconsistency. Ensuring AI output matches personal style preserves the coherent identity that relationships require.

The standard is whether the customer would feel deceived if they knew how the message was created. A personalized message that the salesperson reviewed, edited, and stands behind isn't deceptive even if AI generated the initial draft. A message the salesperson sent without reading would feel deceptive regardless of who created it.

The Uncanny Valley Problem

Personalization that's almost right but not quite triggers stronger negative reaction than no personalization at all. This uncanny valley effect occurs when communication signals understanding but then reveals its limitations. Consider an email that opens with accurate reference to the recipient's company and role, then pivots to generic content that could apply to anyone. The personalized opening creates expectation of personal attention. The generic body reveals that expectation was false. The contrast is jarring. A purely generic email would have set no expectations and created no betrayal. Other uncanny valley triggers include:

Wrong details in personalized frames. "I noticed you recently [thing that didn't happen]" destroys credibility immediately. AI systems pulling from imperfect data sometimes get facts wrong. These errors embedded in personalized language feel worse than generic language would.

Overly formal personalization. "Dear [First Name], as the [Job Title] at [Company Name], you must face [Industry Challenge]" reads as what it is: a template with fields filled in. The mechanical feel undermines the personal intent.

Irrelevant personalization. Referencing something about the recipient that has nothing to do with the message topic feels like surveillance rather than attention. Mentioning someone's college or hometown in a business context without any connecting relevance creates discomfort.

Inconsistent knowledge display. Demonstrating detailed knowledge in one area while being obviously ignorant in another signals incomplete attention. If the message knows about the company's recent acquisition but doesn't know who the recipient reports to, the inconsistency raises questions.

Avoiding the uncanny valley requires quality control on AI personalization. Better to send less personalized communication than communication that fails to deliver on the personalization it attempts. Human review should catch elements that will feel off to recipients.

Customer Perception Management

Different customers have different reactions to AI in sales relationships. Managing these perceptions requires reading each customer and adapting accordingly. Some customers embrace AI as evidence of sophistication. They work in technical fields, appreciate innovation, and see AI adoption as a positive signal about vendor capability. For these customers, visible AI use might actually increase confidence. Other customers prefer traditional human interaction. They chose to work with a salesperson rather than buying through self-service channels because they want human relationship. For these customers, visible AI might feel like downgrade or displacement of the personal attention they valued.

Most customers fall somewhere in between. They appreciate efficiency and capability without thinking much about what tools enable them. They don't need disclosure but won't be upset by it either. They care about outcomes more than methods. Reading these preferences requires the same attentiveness that good sales always requires. Listen for cues about how customers view technology generally. Notice reactions when AI-related topics arise. Adjust how you discuss your tools based on what will resonate with each customer. For customers who clearly prefer human interaction, emphasize the human elements of your approach. The AI assists, but the relationship is with you. For customers who embrace technology, discuss your capabilities openly and even enthusiastically. For the majority in between, focus on results and let process details remain in the background unless they become relevant.

Grace sells human resources software to mid-sized companies. Her customers range from HR directors at technology firms who understand AI deeply to family business owners who distrust anything automated. She adjusts her approach accordingly. With technology-oriented buyers, she discusses how AI helps her identify their likely challenges before they even describe them. With technology-skeptical buyers, she emphasizes her personal attention and availability, mentioning tools only as things that help her serve more attentively. Both approaches are honest. They're just calibrated to what each customer values.

Positioning AI as Customer Benefit

The framing of AI use matters. AI positioned as cost-cutting or efficiency for the seller feels different from AI positioned as service improvement for the customer. Both may be true. Emphasis shapes perception. Customer-benefit framing connects AI capabilities to outcomes customers care about. "Our systems help me catch issues before they become problems" positions monitoring as service. "I can prepare more thoroughly because research that used to take hours now takes minutes" positions efficiency as attention. "We track patterns across our customer base so I can share what's working for companies like yours" positions analytics as insight.

Seller-benefit framing, even if accurate, creates different perception. "AI helps us handle more accounts per salesperson" might be true but doesn't give customers reason to appreciate the technology. It positions them as efficiency targets rather than service recipients. The positioning isn't just about what you say. It's about what you actually do. If AI efficiency gets reinvested in customer service, customers will notice the improved service regardless of what you say about AI. If AI efficiency gets pocketed as cost savings while service quality remains flat, positioning rhetoric won't convince customers otherwise. The authentic path connects AI capability to genuine customer benefit and lets results speak alongside words. Customers who receive better service, faster response, more relevant recommendations, and more reliable follow-through will appreciate the result even if they never think about what enabled it.

Managing AI Mistakes

AI systems make mistakes. They pull incorrect data. They misread signals. They generate inappropriate content. When these mistakes reach customers, trust is at stake. The response to AI mistakes matters more than the mistakes themselves. Handled well, mistakes become opportunities to demonstrate character. Handled poorly, they confirm fears about automation displacing human attention. Several principles guide good response to AI errors.

Take responsibility. Blaming AI for mistakes doesn't work. The salesperson chose to use AI and chose to let its output reach the customer. "Our system got that wrong" is still the salesperson's responsibility. Customers don't care about internal attribution. They care that something wrong happened in their relationship with the salesperson.

Correct promptly. When errors are discovered, fix them quickly. A fast correction signals attention. A slow correction signals indifference. If the error matters enough to address at all, address it immediately.

Over-correct visibly. After AI errors, increase visible human attention. Send a genuinely personal message. Make a phone call you wouldn't have otherwise made. Show that the error triggered increased attention rather than just automated correction. This response can actually strengthen relationships by demonstrating the human backup behind technological capability.

Fix systematically. Some AI errors reflect systemic issues that will recur. Beyond correcting individual instances, address root causes. If AI is pulling from bad data, fix the data. If it's generating inappropriate content, adjust the parameters. Customer-facing errors should trigger process improvement.

Know when to disable. If AI is producing too many errors in a particular context, turn it off. Better to do things manually than to automate mistakes. Human attention applied directly beats AI assistance that's hurting more than helping.

AI mistakes also provide useful information about where human oversight is most needed. Pay attention to error patterns. Apply more human review to the contexts where AI tends to fail. Use mistakes as data for improving the human-AI partnership.

Building Trust Through Competence

Trust has multiple dimensions. One dimension is character: does this person act with integrity? Another dimension is competence: can this person actually deliver? AI affects both dimensions, but its impact on perceived competence is often underappreciated. AI capability can enhance perceived competence in several ways.

Better preparation. A salesperson who shows up deeply informed about the customer's situation signals competence. AI-enabled preparation produces this effect. The customer may not know that AI helped compile the briefing. They just know the salesperson seems to understand their business.

Faster response. Quick turnaround on requests signals capability. When AI helps salespeople respond same-day to questions that would previously have taken a week to research, customers experience that as competence.

Comprehensive knowledge. Drawing on broader information during conversations signals expertise. AI that surfaces relevant data during discussions helps salespeople demonstrate knowledge they might not have recalled on their own.

Reliable follow-through. Keeping commitments consistently signals organizational capability. AI systems that track commitments and ensure nothing falls through cracks make this consistency possible at scale.

Accurate predictions. Being right about customer needs, market developments, and outcome expectations signals business acumen. AI analysis that improves prediction accuracy enhances this perception.

These competence signals build trust alongside character signals. Customers trust salespeople who can actually deliver, not just salespeople with good intentions. AI capability that improves delivery improves the trust that follows from demonstrated competence. The key is that AI-enabled competence must be genuine, not performed. Customers will eventually test capabilities through actual delivery. AI that helps salespeople appear capable initially but can't sustain performance through delivery creates worse outcomes than never having raised expectations.

The Long Game

Trust built on authentic foundation compounds over time. Trust built on false impression collapses when tested. This long-term dynamic should shape how salespeople approach AI and transparency. Short-term optimization tempts salespeople toward practices that maximize immediate response at the expense of sustainable trust. AI makes some of these practices easier. Mass personalization that seems personal but isn't. Aggressive scheduling automation that creates artificial urgency. Engagement tactics that manipulate attention.

These approaches might produce near-term results. They don't build relationships that last. Customers who feel manipulated eventually disengage or retaliate through reduced loyalty, negative references, or active resistance. The alternative is using AI to deliver genuine value that builds authentic relationships. Better preparation makes conversations more valuable for customers. Faster response respects their time. Improved follow-through demonstrates reliability. Enhanced recommendations provide genuine help. These benefits create sustainable trust because they're real. The salespeople who build lasting careers in an AI-enabled world will be those who use the technology to genuinely serve customers better, not those who use it to manipulate more efficiently. Short-term results might look similar. Long-term outcomes will diverge dramatically.

Earning Trust Daily

Trust isn't established once and maintained automatically. It's earned continuously through consistent behavior across many interactions. AI involvement in these interactions creates daily opportunities to strengthen or weaken trust. Every AI-assisted communication is an opportunity. Does this message deliver real value to the recipient? Does it reflect genuine attention to their situation? Does it advance a relationship or just advance a sales process? These questions apply regardless of how the message was created. Answering them well builds trust. Answering them poorly erodes it.

Every customer interaction is a test. Does the salesperson seem to know what they're talking about? Do they follow through on what they promise? Do they treat the customer as a person or as a target? AI can help with information and follow-through, but it can't make a salesperson treat customers as people. That's a choice renewed in every interaction. The daily discipline of earning trust doesn't change because AI is involved. The fundamentals remain: know your customer, provide genuine value, keep your commitments, tell the truth, and care about their outcomes. AI offers tools that can help with each of these. The motivation to use those tools well must come from the salesperson.

Preparing for the Future

Customer expectations about AI will continue evolving. What seems sophisticated today will become standard tomorrow. What feels transparent now may seem evasive later. Salespeople need to stay attuned to these shifts. This means monitoring how customers react to AI in your industry and adjusting approaches accordingly. It means staying aware of broader cultural conversations about AI and how they might shape customer perception. It means being prepared to increase transparency as AI becomes more prevalent and customers become more curious.

The principles outlined in this chapter should remain stable even as tactics evolve. Authenticity matters. Deception backfires. Customer benefit is the right frame. Competence builds trust alongside character. These fundamentals won't change. How they're applied will continue adapting. The next chapter shifts from relationship management to career management. Building trust with customers is essential, but so is building a career that positions you for success as AI reshapes the sales profession. The skills, positioning, and development priorities that will matter going forward deserve focused attention.

Chapter Nine

Building Your AI-Ready Career

The Career Landscape Shift

Career paths in sales have always required adaptation. The skills that launched careers twenty years ago aren't the same skills that advance careers today. Salespeople who succeeded with cold calling had to learn social selling. Those who mastered relationship selling had to add consultative capabilities. Each generation navigates shifts that reshape what it means to be good at the job.

AI represents the current shift. It's not replacing the fundamentals of sales success, but it's changing how those fundamentals get expressed. The salesperson who can't use AI tools will increasingly find themselves at a disadvantage against competitors who can. The salesperson who understands only AI tools without underlying sales capability will fail when machines can't handle what situations require. The careers that thrive will belong to professionals who combine traditional sales excellence with AI competency. This isn't about choosing one or the other. It's about integrating both. This chapter provides a roadmap for building that integration: what to learn, how to demonstrate capability, and how to position yourself for opportunities that AI is creating.

The Competency Stack

Think of sales competency as a stack with multiple layers. Each layer builds on those below it. Gaps in lower layers undermine capability at higher layers.

Foundation layer: Sales fundamentals. Understanding buyer psychology, communicating value, handling objections, building relationships, and closing deals. These fundamentals haven't changed because AI exists. They remain the base on which everything else rests. A salesperson who lacks fundamentals can't compensate with AI skill.

Second layer: Domain expertise. Knowledge of your product, your market, your customers' industries, and the competitive landscape. This expertise enables credibility with buyers and judgment about what matters in specific situations. AI can provide information, but expertise determines how to use it.

Third layer: Process mastery. Understanding your sales methodology, your organization's systems, and how deals actually progress from lead to close. Process mastery enables consistent execution. AI tools integrate into these processes, so understanding them determines how effectively tools get used.

Fourth layer: AI capability. Knowing what AI can do, how to evaluate tools, how to use them effectively, and how to combine AI assistance with human judgment. This layer amplifies the layers below it. Strong fundamentals plus AI capability produces multiplicative results. Weak fundamentals plus AI capability produces little.

Career development should address all four layers, with appropriate prioritization based on current gaps. A salesperson with strong fundamentals but limited AI capability should prioritize AI learning. A salesperson with AI enthusiasm but weak fundamentals should prioritize basics first.

What AI Competency Actually Means

AI competency for sales professionals isn't the same as AI competency for engineers. You don't need to build models, write code, or understand mathematical foundations. You need working knowledge that enables effective use and evaluation of AI tools in sales contexts. Several capabilities define practical AI competency.

Tool fluency. The ability to use AI tools that are relevant to your work. This means knowing the features, understanding the workflows, and having enough practice that use feels natural rather than effortful. Tool fluency comes from actual use over time, not from reading documentation.

Evaluation skill. The ability to assess whether an AI tool actually delivers value. This means knowing what questions to ask vendors, how to design meaningful tests, and how to interpret results. Many AI tools promise more than they deliver. Evaluation skill protects against wasted investment.

Integration thinking. The ability to see how AI fits into existing workflows. This means understanding where AI helps, where it doesn't, and how to combine AI assistance with human effort effectively. Integration thinking turns tools into capability rather than just features.

Limitation awareness. Understanding what AI can't do protects against misuse. This means recognizing when to trust AI recommendations and when to override them, knowing where human judgment is essential, and avoiding automation of activities that require human attention.

Adaptation capacity. AI capabilities evolve quickly. Tools that are leading today will be superseded. The ability to learn new tools rapidly matters more than deep expertise in any particular tool. Adaptation capacity ensures that AI competency remains current as technology changes.

These capabilities develop through combination of learning and practice. Reading about AI provides conceptual foundation. Using AI tools builds practical skill. Reflecting on what works and what doesn't builds judgment.

Learning Without Drowning

The volume of AI content available is overwhelming. New tools launch constantly. Articles, courses, videos, and podcasts compete for attention. Trying to learn everything leads to learning nothing. Focused learning produces better results than scattered consumption. Several principles guide effective AI learning for sales professionals.

Start with your problems. Rather than trying to understand AI comprehensively, identify specific challenges in your current work and explore how AI might address them. Struggling with prospecting? Focus on AI prospecting tools. Spending too much time on administrative tasks? Focus on automation capabilities. Problem-centered learning is immediately applicable. Learn through use. Abstract understanding without application fades quickly. Hands-on experience with actual tools builds lasting capability. When learning about AI capability, get access to real tools and try them on real work. The friction of actual use teaches what reading cannot.

Go deep on one tool before broad on many. Pick a single AI tool relevant to your work and learn it thoroughly before adding others. Deep familiarity with one tool builds patterns that transfer to learning others. Shallow familiarity with many tools provides less actual capability. Build on fundamentals. Much AI learning for sales can be understood as extensions of things you already know. Lead scoring is quantified qualification. Conversation intelligence is systematic call review. Predictive analytics is pattern-based forecasting. Connecting AI concepts to familiar sales concepts accelerates learning.

Accept partial understanding. You won't grasp everything about how AI tools work technically. That's fine. You don't need to understand the engineering to use the capability. Accept that some mechanics will remain black boxes and focus on understanding inputs, outputs, and appropriate applications. Learn from peers. Other sales professionals experimenting with AI tools can share practical insights that formal training misses. What actually worked? What pitfalls emerged? How did they integrate tools into their workflow? Peer learning provides actionable guidance that generic content doesn't.

Demonstrating Capability

AI competency matters for career advancement only if others recognize it. Learning that remains invisible provides limited career benefit. Demonstrating capability makes competency visible to employers, clients, and colleagues. Several approaches demonstrate AI capability effectively. Nothing establishes competency like outcomes. If you use AI tools to improve your numbers, the numbers speak for you. Document how AI contributed to wins. Track metrics before and after AI adoption. Results create credibility that credentials can't match. Beyond results, sharing knowledge establishes expertise. Teaching others through internal documentation about tools you've mastered, presentations to colleagues about what you've learned, and contributions to team training on AI capabilities deepens your own understanding while positioning you as someone who knows the material.

When your organization adopts new AI tools, volunteer to be an early adopter, pilot participant, or implementation champion. Leading implementation positions you at the intersection of technology and sales practice. It also builds relationships with technology leadership who influence career opportunities. As you develop these skills, let colleagues see how you use AI in your work. When someone asks how you prepared so thoroughly for a meeting, explain your AI-assisted research process. When people notice your follow-up consistency, describe the systems that enable it. Visible workflow demonstrates competency without boasting.

Beyond tactical skill, develop and share informed perspective on AI in sales. What's working? What's overhyped? Where is the technology heading? Having thoughtful perspective positions you as someone who understands the landscape, not just someone who uses tools. Remember that AI capability demonstrated once can become stale. Continuous learning and ongoing demonstration of current knowledge maintain the positioning. The person known for AI expertise three years ago who hasn't kept up loses that positioning to others who have.

Positioning for Opportunity

AI is creating new roles, changing existing roles, and shifting what organizations value. Understanding these shifts helps you position for emerging opportunities. Organizations increasingly need people who bridge sales execution and technology implementation. Titles like sales technology specialist, revenue operations analyst, or AI enablement manager represent roles that didn't exist a few years ago. Sales professionals with AI competency can pursue these hybrid positions that pure salespeople or pure technologists can't fill. Related to this, implementation expertise grows in value as organizations adopt AI tools. They need people who can make those tools work in sales contexts. Knowing both the sales process and the technology creates unique implementation capability. Becoming the person who can get AI tools actually adopted and used effectively creates career opportunities beyond traditional quota-carrying roles.

Training demand is also increasing. Organizations adopting AI sales tools need trainers who understand both the technology and how salespeople actually work. The salesperson who becomes skilled at helping others develop AI competency finds career options in enablement, training, and consulting roles. Consulting opportunities are expanding as well. As AI reshapes sales, companies need guidance on strategy and implementation. Former practitioners with demonstrated AI success can move into consulting roles that leverage their combined sales and technology expertise.

Leadership paths are evolving in response to these changes. Sales leadership increasingly requires understanding how to build and manage AI-augmented teams. The path to VP of Sales or Chief Revenue Officer now runs through demonstrated ability to leverage AI for team performance. Future leaders need the competency today. Positioning for these opportunities requires deliberate action. Build the competencies that new roles require. Take assignments that develop relevant experience. Network with people in positions you aspire to reach. Make your interest in emerging opportunities known to those who influence career decisions.

The Bridge Role

Many organizations struggle to connect AI tools with sales practice. Technology teams implement features. Sales teams don't adopt them effectively. The gap between capability and utilization represents a chronic problem. Sales professionals with AI competency can serve as bridges across this gap. They understand what salespeople need because they are salespeople. They understand what technology can provide because they've developed AI competency. This dual understanding enables translation that neither pure technologists nor pure salespeople can provide.

The bridge role involves several functions that create value for the organization. Requirements translation connects sales problems to technology solutions. Sales teams have problems they want solved.

Technology teams have solutions they can build. Bridging means translating sales problems into technology requirements that developers can act on, and translating technology capabilities into practical applications that salespeople can use. Adoption facilitation recognizes that tools don't create value until people use them. Bridging means helping salespeople understand how tools fit their work, addressing resistance, and supporting the behavior change that adoption requires. This facilitation draws on sales skills of persuasion and relationship alongside technology understanding.

Feedback channeling ensures that once tools are in use, information about what's working and what isn't flows to development teams. Bridging means collecting meaningful feedback from salespeople, synthesizing it into actionable insights, and communicating to technology teams in terms they can use. Continuous improvement extends the bridge role beyond initial implementation to ongoing optimization. As tools evolve and sales needs change, someone needs to maintain alignment. This ongoing work creates durable value and job security.

Patrick started as a quota-carrying account executive selling software to retail companies. When his company implemented a new AI-powered prospecting platform, adoption stalled. Salespeople found it confusing and didn't trust the recommendations. Patrick volunteered to help. He worked with the technology team to understand what the tool actually did, then developed training materials that connected those capabilities to the problems his fellow salespeople faced. He ran coaching sessions. He gathered feedback and brought it to product development. Within six months, the company created a new role for him: sales technology lead. He still carries a reduced quota but spends half his time bridging sales and technology teams. His compensation increased and his career trajectory changed.

Building Your Development Plan

Career development happens through intentional action, not passive hope. A development plan turns career aspirations into concrete steps. The process begins with honest assessment of your current capabilities across the competency stack. Where are your strengths? Where are your gaps? What does your current role require? What would advancement require? Assessment provides the baseline from which planning begins. From there, define your target state. What role do you want in two years? Five years? What competencies does that role require? What experiences would prepare you for it? Target state definition provides direction for development activities.

Comparing current state to target state reveals gaps that development should address. Maybe you need stronger AI competency. Maybe you need deeper domain expertise. Maybe you need leadership experience. The gaps prioritize what to work on. For each priority gap, identify activities that will build capability. These might include courses, certifications, stretch assignments, mentoring relationships, or self-directed practice. Effective development uses multiple approaches rather than relying on any single method.

Development activities that aren't scheduled don't happen. Block time for learning. Set deadlines for milestones. Create accountability through commitments to others. Execution turns plans into progress. Periodically assess progress against the plan. What's working? What isn't? Have circumstances changed? Are targets still appropriate? Regular review keeps development aligned with evolving reality.

A development plan for AI competency might include taking an online course on AI fundamentals this quarter, getting certified on your company's primary AI sales tool next quarter, volunteering to pilot a new tool the quarter after that, and presenting learnings to the team by year-end. The specific activities matter less than having concrete steps with timelines.

Managing Career Risk

AI creates career risk alongside career opportunity. Some sales roles will diminish or disappear. Some skills will become less valuable. Managing this risk requires clear-eyed assessment of where you stand. Start by evaluating your current role's trajectory. Is your role moving toward greater AI augmentation or toward AI replacement? Roles involving routine information transfer, simple transaction processing, or basic inquiry handling face higher replacement risk. Roles involving complex relationships, strategic judgment, and creative problem-solving face lower risk. Understanding your role's trajectory informs career decisions. From there, focus on developing portable skills. The specific tools you use today will change. The employer you work for today might not exist in ten years. Skills that transfer across tools, companies, and contexts provide security that role-specific expertise doesn't. Focus on capabilities that remain valuable regardless of which particular AI tools prevail.

Relationships create opportunity when situations change. The people who can recommend you, connect you to openings, or partner with you on new ventures provide resilience against career disruption. Investment in relationships is investment in career security. Financial buffer matters too, because career transitions are easier to navigate with reserves. The ability to take time for retraining, accept a temporarily lower-paying role with better trajectory, or wait for the right opportunity depends on not needing the next paycheck immediately. Financial buffer provides career flexibility.

Stay visible throughout your career. Layoffs and reorganizations typically affect people who are least visible. Visibility creates protection. Make sure decision-makers know who you are, what you contribute, and what you're capable of. Visibility isn't self-promotion. It's ensuring that your value is recognized. Finally, have a backup plan. What would you do if your current role disappeared? Having thought through alternatives reduces anxiety and enables faster response if change becomes necessary. The backup plan might never be needed. Having it provides security.

The Mindset That Sustains

Beyond specific skills and plans, career success with AI requires a mindset that sustains motivation and adaptation over time. Curiosity serves better than fear. AI development will continue surprising everyone. New capabilities will emerge that seem disruptive. A mindset of curiosity treats these developments as interesting rather than threatening. What can this do? How might I use it? What does it mean? Curiosity engages productively with change that fear resists unproductively. Alongside curiosity, a growth orientation outperforms a fixed view of ability. Some people believe their capabilities are set in stone. Others believe capabilities develop through effort. Research consistently shows that the growth mindset leads to better outcomes, especially during periods of change. You can learn AI skills. You can develop new capabilities. You're not limited by where you start.

Contribution matters more than credit. Careers advance through contribution that others value. Focusing on what you give rather than what recognition you receive builds the reputation and relationships that create opportunity. Helping your team succeed with AI, even when you don't get individual recognition, positions you for opportunities that self-focused colleagues miss. Similarly, long-term thinking outperforms short-term optimization. AI-related career decisions should consider multi-year horizons, not just immediate impacts. A role that teaches valuable skills might be worth a short-term pay cut. An assignment that builds critical experience might be worth temporary inconvenience. Short-term optimization often conflicts with long-term success. Finally, resilience beats rigidity. Plans will need adjustment. Setbacks will occur. Unexpected changes will disrupt expectations. Resilience means adapting to these developments rather than breaking against them. The career that succeeds with AI won't follow a straight path. It will navigate through whatever emerges.

Investing in Yourself

Your most valuable career asset is yourself. Investment in your own capability produces returns that compound over time, and this investment takes multiple forms. Time spent learning builds knowledge. Practice builds skill. Experiences build judgment. Relationships build network. Health and energy enable sustained performance. Each form of investment contributes to career capability that grows stronger over years.

The investment must be ongoing because a single burst of learning followed by years of coasting doesn't maintain competitiveness. The environment keeps changing. Competitors keep developing. Staying current requires continuous investment. It also requires protection. Burnout destroys capability, and unsustainable pace eventually collapses. Investment in rest, recovery, and renewal isn't optional. It's part of maintaining the asset base on which career success depends.

Justine has worked in sales for fifteen years. She saw colleagues whose careers stalled when they stopped developing. She also saw colleagues who burned out by pushing too hard without recovery. Her approach balances growth with sustainability. She dedicates five hours weekly to learning, split between AI topics and broader professional development. She protects time for exercise and family that maintain her energy. She's not the fastest learner or the hardest worker. She's consistent and durable. Her career has progressed steadily because she's invested in herself steadily.

Putting Skills to the Test

The skills and positioning discussed in this chapter prepare you for career success in an AI-augmented sales environment. But career development happens through application, not just preparation. The capabilities you build must be deployed in actual sales situations where results matter. Few situations test sales capability more directly than negotiation. When you're across the table from a buyer working to maximize their position while you work to maximize yours, everything comes together: preparation, strategy, real-time adaptation, and human judgment under pressure. Negotiation is where AI assistance and human skill must integrate seamlessly to produce outcomes. The next chapter examines how AI transforms negotiation, from the intelligence gathering that precedes it to the analysis that follows. Understanding how to leverage AI in these high-stakes moments while preserving the human judgment that negotiation requires is essential for any salesperson seeking to maximize deal value.

Chapter Ten

AI in Complex Negotiations

Where Stakes Are Highest

Negotiation is where sales outcomes are determined. Everything that precedes it, the prospecting, the discovery, the presentations, and the relationship building, creates the opportunity. Negotiation decides what that opportunity is worth. The difference between a good negotiation and a poor one can mean tens of thousands of dollars on a single deal and millions across a career. High stakes demand high preparation. The best negotiators don't just show up with charm and instincts. They arrive with deep understanding of the other party's position, clear strategy for their own approach, and contingency plans for multiple scenarios. This preparation has always separated successful negotiators from those who leave value on the table.

AI transforms what's possible in negotiation preparation, real-time support, and post-negotiation learning. It processes information that humans can't gather manually. It identifies patterns that humans wouldn't notice. It suggests approaches based on what has worked in similar situations. The salesperson who integrates AI into their negotiation practice operates at a different level than one who relies solely on experience and instinct. But negotiation remains fundamentally human. Reading the room, building rapport, knowing when to push and when to yield, and managing the emotional dynamics of the conversation require capabilities AI doesn't possess. The goal isn't replacing human negotiation skill with AI. It's augmenting human skill to produce better outcomes.

Intelligence Gathering

Negotiation success begins long before the negotiation starts. Understanding the other party's situation, constraints, and likely positions shapes strategy. The more you know, the better you can prepare. Traditional intelligence gathering relies on limited sources: what the customer has told you, what's publicly available about their company, and whatever your network can provide. This information is useful but incomplete. You're working with fragments rather than a full picture. AI expands intelligence gathering dramatically. It synthesizes information across sources that humans couldn't practically monitor or integrate.

Company analysis pulls together financial data, strategic initiatives, recent announcements, executive statements, and market position. AI can process earnings calls, investor presentations, industry reports, and news coverage to build a comprehensive picture of the customer's business situation. A company under margin pressure negotiates differently than one flush with cash. A company pursuing aggressive growth has different priorities than one focused on cost control. Stakeholder mapping identifies the people involved in the decision and what's known about each. LinkedIn profiles, published articles, speaking appearances, and social media activity reveal professional backgrounds, stated priorities, and communication styles. Understanding who you're negotiating with provides advantage over going in blind.

Competitive intelligence reveals what alternatives the customer is likely considering and how those alternatives compare. AI can monitor competitor pricing, product changes, and customer feedback to inform how your offer stacks up. Knowing what the customer can get elsewhere shapes what you need to offer. Historical pattern analysis examines past negotiations with this customer or similar customers. What terms did they prioritize? Where did they push hardest? What concessions did they accept? Patterns from previous deals inform expectations for the current one.

Relationship history compiles everything your organization knows about this customer: past purchases, support interactions, satisfaction indicators, and relationship dynamics. This institutional memory prevents you from starting fresh when you should be building on what's known. The assembled intelligence creates a foundation for strategic preparation that raw human effort can't match. A negotiator entering a meeting with AI-powered briefing knows more about the other party than any human could reasonably gather through manual research.

Pricing Optimization

Price is usually the most contested element in negotiation. Customers push for lower prices. Sellers resist. The outcome depends on leverage, skill, and preparation on both sides. AI contributes to pricing strategy in several ways that strengthen the seller's position.

Price sensitivity modeling estimates how customers will respond to different price points. Based on customer characteristics, historical patterns, and market conditions, AI predicts which customers will accept higher prices and which require discounting to close. This modeling informs initial pricing and discount strategy. Competitive price positioning extends this analysis by tracking where your pricing falls relative to alternatives. AI can estimate competitor pricing from various signals and help you understand how your offer compares. Knowing you're priced fifteen percent above the primary alternative creates different negotiation dynamics than knowing you're priced below.

Value quantification helps translate product benefits into financial terms customers can evaluate. AI can analyze customer data to estimate the specific value your solution would provide to this particular buyer. A proposal that demonstrates $500,000 in annual savings justifies premium pricing more effectively than one that lists features without financial context. Deal structure optimization explores alternative ways to package offers that might break impasses. Maybe the customer resists upfront pricing but would accept higher total contract value spread over time. Maybe they need certain terms for budget reasons that don't actually cost you much. AI can model different structures to identify options that work for both parties. Discount impact analysis adds another layer by calculating what different discount levels actually cost in profitability and precedent. A ten percent discount sounds small, but its impact on margin might be substantial. Understanding the real cost of concessions informs how hard to resist them.

Sandra sells enterprise software with complex pricing structures. Before a major contract negotiation, she uses AI analysis to model twelve different pricing scenarios. The analysis reveals that shifting from perpetual licensing to subscription actually increases total contract value over five years despite a lower annual payment. It also shows that the customer's publicly stated budget constraints are looser than their negotiating position suggests, based on their recent technology investments. She enters the negotiation with options and intelligence that reshape the conversation from the start.

Scenario Planning

Negotiations rarely follow predicted paths. The other party raises unexpected issues. Offers get rejected. New stakeholders appear with different priorities. Effective negotiators prepare for multiple scenarios rather than single outcomes. AI enhances scenario planning by simulating possible negotiation paths and their likely results.

Alternative outcome modeling maps what happens under different negotiation scenarios. If you concede on price, what's the impact on margin? If you hold firm, what's the probability of deal loss? If you offer extended payment terms, how does that affect cash flow? These calculations inform which battles to fight and which to concede. Concession strategy planning builds on this foundation, determining what to give up and in what order. AI can analyze historical negotiations to identify which concessions typically satisfy customers with minimum cost to the seller, suggesting sequences that preserve margin while maintaining deal momentum.

Walk-away analysis clarifies your actual alternatives if the negotiation fails. What other opportunities exist for this sales capacity? What's the real cost of losing this deal versus accepting unfavorable terms? AI can quantify the walk-away scenario to inform how much risk to accept. Stakeholder reaction prediction adds another layer, anticipating how different people involved will respond to various approaches. Based on what's known about each stakeholder's priorities and style, AI can suggest which arguments will resonate with whom and what concerns are likely to arise.

The output isn't a script to follow rigidly. It's a strategic foundation that enables more flexible and confident response to whatever actually happens. The negotiator who has thought through multiple scenarios adapts more effectively than one who prepared for only a single path.

Real-Time Support

Negotiation happens in real time. You can't pause to research while the customer waits. The moment demands immediate response. Traditional preparation helps, but it can't cover every situation that arises. Emerging AI capabilities provide real-time support during live negotiations that addresses this challenge.

Information retrieval accesses relevant data on demand. When the customer mentions a specific competitor, concern, or requirement, AI can pull relevant information for the negotiator to reference. This retrieval happens fast enough to inform the live conversation. Conversation tracking maintains awareness of what's been discussed, what's been agreed, and what remains unresolved. In complex negotiations with multiple issues, losing track of the details is easy. AI can maintain comprehensive notes that the negotiator reviews between topics or during breaks. Sentiment monitoring detects emotional shifts in the conversation, providing signals about whether the customer is becoming frustrated, warming to your position, or reacting to a sensitive issue. AI analysis of tone and language supplements the negotiator's own reading of the room. Recommendation prompting suggests tactics based on how the conversation is developing. If the customer has raised a specific objection three times, AI might prompt the negotiator to address it more directly. If an opportunity to close seems to be opening, AI might suggest asking for commitment.

These real-time capabilities require appropriate interfaces. A negotiator can't stare at a laptop screen while trying to build rapport. The most effective implementations use subtle delivery methods: an earpiece, a smartwatch vibration, or a brief glance at a secondary screen during natural pauses. Throughout, the human negotiator remains in control. AI provides information and suggestions. The negotiator decides what to use and how. The combination of human judgment and AI support produces better outcomes than either alone.

Pattern Recognition Across Negotiations

Individual negotiations generate learning. Experienced negotiators develop intuitions about what works based on accumulated practice. But human learning from experience is limited by memory, attention, and cognitive bias. We remember vivid examples more than typical ones. We attribute success to favored tactics even when the evidence is ambiguous.

AI pattern recognition across many negotiations produces more reliable insights. Success factor identification determines which behaviors and approaches correlate with better outcomes. Across thousands of negotiations, AI can identify patterns: opening with a specific type of discussion leads to better results, addressing price early versus late affects outcomes, certain language patterns predict deal closure. These patterns inform training and strategy. Objection analysis reveals which objections arise most frequently and which responses prove most effective. Rather than developing objection handling from anecdote, negotiators can draw on statistical evidence about what actually works.

Timing patterns show when negotiations tend to succeed or fail. Are deals closed faster when momentum builds early? Do negotiations that stall past certain points rarely recover? AI analysis of timing provides guidance on pacing and when to escalate urgency. Individual benchmarking compares your negotiation patterns to successful peers. Are you talking too much? Conceding too quickly? Missing opportunities to advance? AI can identify how your approach differs from what works for top performers.

Organizations that capture and analyze negotiation data build institutional knowledge that individual experience can't match. New negotiators learn faster by accessing insights from the collective experience. Experienced negotiators improve by discovering patterns they hadn't consciously recognized.

Preparation Workflows

Integrating AI into negotiation preparation requires systematic workflow rather than occasional tool use. Pre-negotiation briefing generation should happen automatically before significant negotiations. The system knows which meetings are coming and can prepare relevant intelligence without manual request. The negotiator reviews the briefing rather than requesting it. Strategy development sessions then combine AI analysis with human judgment. AI provides data about the customer, the competitive situation, and historical patterns. The human negotiator uses this input to develop strategy that reflects context AI doesn't fully understand: relationship nuances, organizational politics, and strategic considerations beyond the individual deal.

Rehearsal and simulation allow negotiators to practice with AI-powered scenarios. The system plays the customer role, raising objections and testing responses. This simulation helps negotiators prepare for difficult moments before facing them in live situations. Playbook integration connects AI recommendations to established negotiation approaches. Rather than generic suggestions, AI guidance reflects your organization's specific priorities. The system knows what your company's negotiation philosophy is and aligns recommendations accordingly. For complex negotiations involving multiple people, AI can help with team coordination, clarifying who addresses which topics, what each person's role is, and how to hand off smoothly between team members. Effective preparation workflows make AI assistance systematic rather than sporadic. The goal is ensuring every significant negotiation benefits from available AI capability without requiring extra effort to access it.

Post-Negotiation Analysis

Negotiations generate learning opportunities that often go unexploited. The deal closes or fails. Everyone moves on to the next priority. What could be learned from what just happened gets lost. AI enables systematic post-negotiation analysis that captures learning for future benefit.

Outcome analysis compares what was achieved to what was possible. Was more value left on the table? Were concessions made that weren't necessary? AI can analyze the final deal terms against benchmarks to identify opportunities for improvement in future negotiations. Conversation analysis examines how the negotiation actually unfolded, revealing what topics consumed the most time, where the discussion got stuck, and what moments seemed to shift the dynamic. Recording and analyzing negotiations reveals patterns not visible in the moment.

Prediction accuracy assessment evaluates whether pre-negotiation intelligence proved accurate. Did the customer behave as expected? Were anticipated objections raised? Did the predicted pressure points actually matter? This assessment improves future intelligence gathering by identifying what to weight more or less heavily. Strategy effectiveness review determines whether the planned approach worked. Did the concession strategy play out as designed? Did the value proposition resonate as expected? Did timing recommendations prove sound? Reviewing strategy against results builds better playbooks. Action item tracking ensures that commitments made during negotiation get fulfilled. Negotiations often involve promises about implementation, support, or follow-up. AI can capture these commitments and track them to completion.

Organizations that systematically analyze negotiations improve faster than those that don't. Each deal becomes input for better performance on future deals. Over time, this learning compounds into significant negotiation capability advantage.

The Human Core of Negotiation

With all that AI contributes, negotiation remains fundamentally human. Certain elements require capabilities AI doesn't possess. Relationship dynamics shape negotiation more than logic alone. People do business with people they trust and like. Building rapport, demonstrating respect, and managing interpersonal tension are human skills. AI can't make someone like you or trust you. That's work you have to do yourself. Reading non-verbal cues provides information that words don't convey. A pause before answering, a glance between stakeholders, posture shifts when certain topics arise. These signals reveal what the other party is thinking beyond what they're saying. AI can analyze recordings after the fact, but in-the-moment reading remains human.

Creative problem-solving breaks through impasses when standard approaches don't work. Finding novel solutions requires creativity that AI doesn't possess. The unexpected offer that reframes the discussion, the connection nobody else saw, the creative structure that meets both parties' needs: these breakthroughs come from human insight. Judgment about when to push and when to yield requires wisdom that experience builds. Calculations can inform this judgment, but the decision itself requires human assessment of factors that can't be fully quantified. Is this relationship worth protecting at the cost of this deal's margin? Is this the moment to make a stand or a moment for strategic concession? Ethical navigation also arises when negotiation tactics approach manipulation. Where is the line between persuasion and deception? When does aggressive negotiation become bad faith? These ethical judgments require values and conscience that AI lacks. The most effective negotiators combine AI capability with human skill. They use AI for what it does well: gathering intelligence, modeling scenarios, analyzing patterns, and providing real-time information. They contribute what only humans can: building relationships, reading situations, exercising judgment, and navigating complexity with creativity and integrity.

Avoiding Common Pitfalls

AI-assisted negotiation can go wrong in predictable ways. Awareness of common pitfalls helps avoid them. Over-reliance on data can make negotiators rigid. When the data says one thing but the situation feels different, human judgment should prevail. Data informs but doesn't dictate. The negotiator who overrules their instincts because the model says otherwise often regrets it. Information overload presents a related challenge, overwhelming rather than helping. AI can produce more intelligence than anyone can absorb. The goal is relevant information, not maximum information. Curation of what reaches the negotiator matters as much as generation. Analysis paralysis delays action while seeking more preparation. There's always more analysis that could be done. At some point, you have to negotiate with what you know. Preparation has diminishing returns, and delay has costs.

Mechanical execution of AI recommendations feels inauthentic. If you're clearly following a script or checklist, the other party notices. AI recommendations should be internalized and adapted to the moment, not recited. Perhaps most damaging, neglecting relationship for transaction undermines long-term outcomes. AI analysis tends to focus on deal terms rather than relationship quality. But the relationship often matters more than any single deal. Winning every point while damaging the relationship is losing in disguise. These pitfalls aren't arguments against AI use. They're reminders that AI is a tool requiring judgment to use well. The negotiator remains responsible for outcomes and for integrating AI assistance appropriately.

The Integration Imperative

Negotiation capability increasingly depends on integrating AI assistance with human skill. Salespeople who negotiate without AI support are disadvantaged against those who have it. Organizations that don't build AI negotiation capability fall behind competitors who do. This integration requires investment at individual and organizational levels. Individual negotiators must learn to use AI tools effectively. Organizations must build data infrastructure that enables AI analysis, create workflows that make AI assistance systematic, and develop training that helps negotiators combine AI capability with human skill.

The investment pays off in measurable terms: better deal outcomes, more efficient negotiation processes, and faster improvement through systematic learning. The negotiation advantage that AI provides compounds over time as organizations accumulate data and refine their approaches. But individuals can't build this capability alone. It requires organizational support: tools, training, data, and leadership commitment. The question of how to lead AI-augmented sales teams, including how to build negotiation capability across teams rather than just in individuals, becomes central to organizational success.

The next chapter examines sales leadership in the AI era. It addresses how to build, develop, and direct teams that leverage AI effectively, including how to develop negotiation capability and other AI-augmented skills across your entire sales organization rather than just in exceptional individuals.

Chapter Eleven

Leading AI-Augmented Sales Teams

The Leadership Challenge

Sales leadership has always required balancing competing demands: driving short-term results while building long-term capability, pushing for productivity while maintaining morale, standardizing processes while allowing individual adaptation. AI adds new dimensions to this balancing act without eliminating the old ones.

Leaders of AI-augmented teams face questions their predecessors didn't encounter. How do you hire for a future where AI capability matters but doesn't yet exist in most candidates? How do you train people on tools that keep changing? How do you set performance expectations when AI makes some things easier and other things more important? How do you coach when AI already provides feedback?

How do you maintain human connection in customer relationships when automation handles more touchpoints?

These questions don't have simple answers. They require leadership judgment applied to specific contexts. But frameworks exist that help leaders think through the challenges and make better decisions. This chapter addresses the leadership dimensions of AI-augmented sales teams. It's written for sales managers, directors, and executives who are responsible not just for their own AI competency but for building AI capability across organizations. The principles apply whether you lead a team of five or an organization of five hundred.

Hiring for AI Readiness

The people you hire today will work in an AI environment that's more developed tomorrow. Hiring for current skills alone produces teams unprepared for where the profession is heading. AI readiness in candidates involves several observable characteristics. Learning agility indicates capacity to master new tools quickly. Candidates who have successfully learned multiple technologies, adapted to changing environments, and demonstrated curiosity about new approaches will adapt to AI tools better than those who haven't. Ask candidates about times they had to learn something unfamiliar quickly. Their answers reveal learning patterns. Comfort with technology provides the foundation for AI tool adoption. This doesn't mean technical expertise. It means ease with digital tools generally. Candidates who resist technology in their personal lives or struggle with basic sales tools will struggle with AI adoption. Observe how candidates interact with technology during the hiring process itself.

Process orientation indicates ability to integrate AI into workflows systematically. AI tools deliver value when used consistently within structured processes. Candidates who approach work methodically, follow systems, and appreciate process discipline will integrate AI more effectively than those who operate purely on instinct. Judgment capability becomes more important as AI handles more routine work. When AI provides analysis and recommendations, humans contribute judgment about what to do with those inputs. Candidates who demonstrate thoughtful decision-making under uncertainty, who can articulate their reasoning, and who know when to trust versus question information possess judgment that AI augments rather than replaces. Relationship orientation indicates focus on the human elements AI can't handle. Candidates who genuinely enjoy connecting with people, building trust, and maintaining long-term relationships will thrive in roles where AI handles transactions and humans handle relationships. Ask candidates about relationships they've built and maintained over time. Hiring for these characteristics doesn't mean ignoring traditional sales competencies. Candidates still need communication skills, drive, resilience, and domain aptitude. AI readiness adds to the evaluation criteria rather than replacing what already matters.

Onboarding for AI Competency

New hires need AI competency from the start. Waiting to train on AI tools until after general onboarding delays capability development and creates habits that don't incorporate AI assistance. Effective AI onboarding integrates tool training with sales process training. Rather than teaching the sales process first and AI tools later, teach them together. Show new hires how AI fits into prospecting from day one. Demonstrate AI-assisted preparation as the standard approach to meetings. Present AI tools as normal parts of how work gets done rather than optional additions.

Early wins with AI tools build positive momentum. Structure initial assignments so that AI assistance produces visible improvement in outcomes. A new hire who uses AI to prepare thoroughly for their first customer meeting and receives positive feedback learns that AI helps. Early negative experiences with AI create resistance that persists. Mentoring relationships should include AI capability transfer. Pair new hires with experienced salespeople who use AI effectively. The mentor demonstrates integration of AI tools into actual work, not just theoretical capability. New hires learn how the best performers actually use AI rather than just what the tools can do. Expectations about AI use should be explicit from the start. If the organization expects salespeople to use AI for research, preparation, and follow-up, state that expectation clearly during onboarding. Vague suggestions that people "might want to try" AI tools produce inconsistent adoption. Clear expectations that AI use is standard practice produce consistent capability.

Training That Sticks

AI tool training often fails. Organizations invest in training programs, salespeople attend sessions, and then nothing changes. The tools don't get used. The capability doesn't develop. The investment produces no return. Effective AI training follows principles that differ from traditional training approaches. Train in workflow context, because abstract tool demonstrations don't transfer to actual work. Training should show how tools fit into specific workflows the salesperson performs daily. Don't train on "how to use the AI research tool." Train on "how to prepare for a discovery call using AI research as part of your standard process." Practice with real work rather than hypothetical scenarios, since training exercises using made-up cases produce less retention than practice on actual deals. Have salespeople use AI tools on their current opportunities during training. The immediate relevance increases engagement and produces work output alongside learning.

Space learning over time because single training sessions produce temporary understanding that fades quickly. Spaced learning with reinforcement over weeks produces lasting capability. Initial training should be followed by check-ins, refreshers, and advanced sessions as proficiency develops. Provide just-in-time support so that when salespeople encounter situations where AI could help, assistance is immediately available. This might mean accessible documentation, chat-based help, or designated experts who can answer questions quickly. Learning happens at the moment of need better than in scheduled sessions.

Measure and reinforce by tracking AI tool usage and connecting it to outcomes. Share data showing that salespeople who use AI tools achieve better results. Recognition for effective AI use reinforces the behavior. Accountability for expected AI use prevents regression. Update training continuously because AI tools evolve quickly. Training that was accurate six months ago may describe features that no longer exist or miss new capabilities. Training programs need continuous updating to remain relevant. Assign ownership for keeping training current.

Coaching in the AI Era

Sales coaching has always involved observation, feedback, and development guidance. AI changes what coaches observe, what feedback is available, and what development looks like. AI provides coaching data that transforms what's possible. Conversation intelligence platforms analyze every call, identifying patterns that human observation would miss. A coach no longer needs to ride along to understand how a salesperson conducts meetings. AI provides talk-time ratios, question patterns, topic coverage, and sentiment analysis across all interactions. This data enables coaching conversations grounded in comprehensive evidence rather than limited samples.

Coaching focus shifts as a result. When AI provides feedback on mechanics, coaches can focus on judgment and strategy. A salesperson can learn from AI analysis that they talk too much during discovery calls. The coach's value-add becomes helping them understand why they talk too much and how to adjust their approach. Coaching becomes more strategic as AI handles tactical feedback. Personalization increases as well. AI analysis reveals individual patterns that generic coaching misses. One salesperson might struggle with objection handling while another handles objections well but fails to ask for commitment. AI identifies specific development needs for each individual. Coaches can provide targeted guidance rather than one-size-fits-all advice.

Self-coaching becomes possible when salespeople have access to AI feedback and can identify their own improvement opportunities. The coach's role shifts toward helping salespeople interpret AI feedback, prioritize development areas, and design practice approaches. Coaching becomes collaborative problem-solving rather than top-down evaluation.

Mitchell manages a team of twelve account managers. Before AI coaching tools, he spent significant time reviewing recorded calls and observing live meetings. Now AI analysis flags specific coaching opportunities across his entire team. He receives alerts when a salesperson's patterns change, such as when suddenly someone's talk-time increases or their question frequency drops. His coaching conversations start with AI-generated insights but focus on understanding root causes and developing solutions. The combination of AI analysis and human coaching produces faster development than either alone achieved.

Setting Performance Expectations

AI changes what's possible, which changes what should be expected. Performance standards that made sense before AI may be too low in an AI-augmented environment. Standards set without considering AI reality may be impossible to achieve without it. Baseline expectations should assume AI use. If AI tools are available and expected to be used, performance standards should reflect what's achievable with AI assistance. A salesperson who can research fifty prospects daily with AI help should be expected to do more prospecting than one who had to research manually. Setting expectations at pre-AI levels leaves productivity gains unrealized. Quality expectations should rise with efficiency. When AI saves time on preparation and administration, that time should go toward higher-quality customer engagement. Expectations for meeting preparation, follow-up thoroughness, and relationship development can increase because time is available for these activities.

Activity metrics need recalibration because traditional metrics like calls made and emails sent measured effort in a pre-AI context. With AI assistance, these activities take less effort, so hitting activity numbers is easier. Metrics should shift toward outcomes and quality rather than raw activity volume. Different performers need different expectations as well. Top performers with AI tools will achieve significantly more than average performers. The gap between high and low performers may widen as AI amplifies existing capability differences. Performance expectations should differentiate rather than applying one standard to all. Expectations should also evolve with capability. As AI tools improve and salespeople become more proficient, expectations should increase accordingly. Static expectations in a dynamic environment either become too easy as capability grows or remain impossible if capability doesn't develop as expected. The principle underlying all these adjustments is that expectations should reflect realistic assessment of what's achievable with the tools and training available. Leaders who understand AI capability can set appropriate expectations. Leaders who don't understand will either expect too much or settle for too little.

Compensation in AI-Augmented Environments

Compensation structures influence behavior. Structures designed for pre-AI selling may produce unintended consequences in AI-augmented environments. The balance between individual versus team contribution deserves consideration. AI tools often benefit from organizational investment: data infrastructure, tool selection, training programs, and process design. Individual salespeople leverage these organizational assets. Compensation that rewards only individual results may undervalue organizational contribution to those results. Some organizations are introducing team-based components that recognize collective investment in AI capability. The tension between efficiency versus effectiveness also matters. When AI makes salespeople more efficient, they can handle more accounts with less effort per account. Compensation based purely on volume might encourage breadth at the expense of depth. If relationship quality matters, compensation should include indicators of account health and customer satisfaction, not just deal count.

Tool adoption incentives can accelerate capability development. During AI adoption phases, some organizations include tool usage in performance evaluation or compensation. This creates explicit incentive to develop AI capability. The approach works best as a temporary measure during transition rather than permanent fixture. Organizations must also consider how to handle windfall effects. Sometimes AI produces results that exceed what any individual effort would have achieved. A predictive lead scoring system might identify opportunities that salespeople would never have found on their own. How should compensation handle these AI-enabled windfalls? Some organizations adjust quota or expectations to account for AI contribution to results. Career progression criteria should evolve as well. Advancement decisions should consider AI capability alongside traditional sales competency. A salesperson who achieves quota but never develops AI proficiency has limited growth potential. Career progression criteria should include demonstrated AI competency and willingness to adopt new capabilities. There's no universal right answer on compensation structure. The right approach depends on your sales model, your culture, and your strategic priorities. But leaders should explicitly consider how AI affects the behaviors their compensation structure encourages.

Maintaining Culture Through Automation

Culture is carried through human interactions. When automation handles more customer touchpoints and AI mediates more internal processes, the interactions that maintain culture become fewer. Leaders must intentionally preserve cultural elements that might otherwise erode. Customer connection culture can weaken when AI handles routine interactions. If salespeople only engage customers for major meetings and negotiations, they lose the relationship maintenance that regular contact provides. Leaders should protect time and create expectations for human customer connection beyond what deals strictly require. Learning culture can weaken when AI provides answers. The habit of inquiry, of asking why things work the way they do, can atrophy when AI just tells you what to do. Leaders should maintain curiosity and learning as cultural values, encouraging people to understand AI recommendations rather than just following them.

Collaboration culture can weaken when AI eliminates some reasons to interact with colleagues. If you can ask AI instead of asking a teammate, you might lose the relationship building that questions create. Leaders should create structures for collaboration that exist regardless of AI capability. Accountability culture can weaken when AI involvement complicates attribution. If a deal was lost, was it the salesperson's fault or the AI's recommendation? If a deal was won, who deserves credit? Leaders must maintain accountability while acknowledging AI's role. Human connection culture is the foundation for everything else. Sales organizations need people who care about each other as people, not just as productivity units. When automation handles more work, the remaining human interactions should be protected as the connective tissue that holds organizations together.

Culture maintenance requires intentional effort from leadership. The forces of efficiency push toward automation of everything that can be automated. Cultural preservation pushes back, protecting human elements that automation would otherwise eliminate. Leaders must actively manage this tension.

Managing Change

AI adoption is a change management challenge. New tools, new processes, and new expectations require people to work differently. Resistance is natural. Managing through resistance determines whether AI investment produces return. Communicate the why, because salespeople adopt change more readily when they understand the reasons. Explain why AI tools are being introduced, what problems they solve, and how they benefit the salespeople themselves. Abstract corporate justifications about efficiency don't motivate. Concrete explanations about how this makes your job easier and your results better do motivate. Involve people in design because change imposed from above generates more resistance than change that people helped shape. Include salespeople in evaluating tools, designing workflows, and planning implementation. Their input improves decisions and their involvement increases commitment.

Start with believers since early adopters who are enthusiastic about AI create momentum. Start implementation with people who want to try new tools. Their success creates evidence that persuades skeptics. Their experience identifies issues to address before broad rollout. Address resistance directly because some resistance reflects legitimate concerns that should be addressed while some reflects fear or preference for the familiar. Distinguish between them. Legitimate concerns about tool limitations or workflow disruption deserve response. Resistance based on general discomfort needs different handling: patience, support, and clear expectations.

Maintain support through the dip because change often produces a temporary performance dip before improvement. New tools take time to learn. New processes take time to become routine. Leaders must support teams through this transition period without abandoning the change effort at the first sign of difficulty. Celebrate wins because success stories reinforce the value of change. When AI tools produce visible wins, recognize them publicly. Share examples of how AI-assisted approaches achieved results that wouldn't have been possible otherwise. Wins create energy for continued change.

Adriana led her organization through an AI adoption initiative that initially met significant resistance. Several senior salespeople saw no reason to change approaches that had worked for years. She addressed resistance by pairing skeptics with early adopters, creating visible evidence of results, and maintaining patient but firm expectations. Within a year, previous skeptics had become advocates who couldn't imagine working without AI assistance. The transition required constant attention and frequent adjustment, but the organization emerged with capability it hadn't possessed before.

Balancing Efficiency and Relationship Quality

AI creates efficiency that enables either more volume or more depth. The choice between them is a leadership decision with significant implications. The volume path uses efficiency gains to expand coverage. Each salesperson handles more accounts. Cost per customer contact decreases. This path makes sense when relationships are transactional, when customers don't expect deep personal attention, and when market opportunity exceeds current coverage.

The depth path uses efficiency gains to enhance relationship quality. Each salesperson maintains the same coverage but invests recovered time in richer customer engagement. This path makes sense when relationships drive differentiation, when customer lifetime value depends on relationship depth, and when competitive advantage comes from trust rather than reach.

Most organizations need a blend. Some customer segments warrant deep relationship investment. Others are better served through efficient, largely automated engagement. The leader's job is determining which approach fits which context and structuring teams accordingly. The danger is letting efficiency dictate depth by default. If efficiency gains get pocketed as cost reduction without deliberate decision about where to reinvest, relationship quality declines by neglect. Leaders must actively decide how efficiency gains get deployed rather than accepting whatever outcome emerges.

Deciding What to Automate

Not everything that can be automated should be. Leaders must decide which activities to automate and which to protect for human attention. Automate when AI does it better. Data entry, scheduling, routine research, and basic inquiry response are often done better by AI than by humans. Speed is faster. Consistency is higher. Error rates are lower. These activities are obvious automation candidates. Automate when human effort adds no value. Some tasks must be done but don't benefit from human touch. Administrative compliance, internal reporting, and process documentation fall into this category. Human attention here has opportunity cost without corresponding benefit.

Protect when human touch creates value. Some activities produce different outcomes when humans do them versus when machines do them. Relationship building, trust development, and complex problem-solving benefit from genuine human engagement. Automating these activities sacrifices value even if it creates efficiency. Protect when learning matters. Some activities develop capability through the doing. A new salesperson who learns to research prospects manually develops understanding that shapes how they use AI research later. Strategic automation of learning activities can stunt development. Protect when customers expect humans. Customer expectations about when they should interact with humans versus machines vary by context and culture. Violating these expectations damages relationships regardless of whether automation would be more efficient. The automation decision isn't binary. Many activities can be partially automated: AI does the heavy lifting, human review ensures quality. Finding the right division of labor for each activity type requires judgment that considers efficiency, quality, customer expectation, and capability development.

Building Organizational Capability

Individual salesperson capability matters, but organizational capability matters more. An organization where AI expertise resides in a few individuals is fragile. An organization with broad, systematic AI capability is durable.

Create centers of expertise by designating people responsible for AI tool mastery, best practice development, and internal support. These experts enable the broader organization to leverage AI without requiring everyone to develop deep expertise. Document and share what works. When someone discovers an effective AI-assisted approach, capture it. Create playbooks, templates, and guides that allow others to replicate success. Organizational learning happens through systematic knowledge sharing.

Build data infrastructure because AI capability depends on data. Organizations with clean, comprehensive, accessible data enable AI applications that organizations with poor data can't support. Investment in data infrastructure is investment in AI capability. Develop feedback loops by creating mechanisms to learn what's working and what isn't. Track tool usage and outcomes. Gather salesperson feedback on AI assistance quality. Use this information to continuously improve AI integration. Plan for continuous evolution because AI capability isn't a destination. It's a journey. Tools will change. Capabilities will expand. Best practices will evolve. Build organizational capacity for ongoing adaptation rather than one-time implementation.

The leader's role in building organizational capability extends beyond directing individual salespeople. It involves creating systems, investing in infrastructure, and shaping culture in ways that enable AI leverage across the entire organization.

The Technology Decisions

Leaders must make decisions about which AI tools to adopt, how to integrate them, and how to manage the technology stack. These decisions have significant implications for team capability and organizational success. Individual salespeople can develop preferences and competencies, but the platform decisions typically happen at the leadership level. Getting these decisions right matters enormously. Getting them wrong can mean wasted investment, failed adoption, and capability disadvantage.

The next chapter examines how to build an effective AI sales stack. It provides frameworks for evaluating tools, selecting platforms, and integrating technologies into coherent capability. Leaders who understand these frameworks make better technology decisions and build stronger AI capability for their organizations.

Chapter Twelve

Building Your AI Sales Stack

The Stack Concept

A sales technology stack is the collection of tools that support sales work. Before AI, this typically meant CRM as the foundation, with various point solutions layered on top for email, phone, proposal generation, and other specific functions. The tools were relatively stable and the integration challenges were manageable. AI has complicated the stack significantly. New categories of tools have emerged. Existing categories have been transformed by AI capability. Integration requirements have become more demanding as AI tools need data from multiple sources to function effectively. The number of vendors claiming AI capability has exploded, making evaluation more difficult.

Building an effective AI sales stack requires systematic thinking about what you need, what's available, how tools work together, and what the true costs are. Random tool adoption based on vendor pitches or competitive pressure produces stacks that don't integrate well, duplicate functionality, and cost more than they're worth. Deliberate stack building produces coherent capability that amplifies sales effectiveness. This chapter provides frameworks for making AI tool decisions. Whether you're responsible for organization-wide technology strategy or just trying to understand the tools available to you, these frameworks help navigate a confusing market.

Categories of AI Sales Tools

The AI sales tool market has grown complex, but tools cluster into recognizable categories based on what they do. CRM and data platforms form the foundation of most sales stacks. Modern CRMs increasingly incorporate AI features: lead scoring, opportunity prediction, activity capture, and recommendation engines. Some organizations build AI capability on top of existing CRM platforms. Others adopt specialized AI platforms that integrate with CRM. Conversation intelligence tools record, transcribe, and analyze sales conversations. They identify patterns in what's said, how it's said, and what predicts success. The category includes call recording platforms, meeting analysis tools, and coaching applications that draw on conversation data.

Sales engagement platforms manage outreach sequences, track responses, and optimize timing and messaging. AI features include send-time optimization, message personalization, and response prediction. These tools sit between CRM and actual customer communication. Prospecting and lead generation tools identify potential customers and provide intelligence about them. AI capabilities include predictive lead scoring, intent signal detection, and automated research compilation. Some focus on finding new prospects while others focus on scoring and prioritizing existing leads.

Content and proposal automation tools generate sales materials tailored to specific opportunities. AI enables personalization at scale, from email drafts to full proposals. The category includes document generation, presentation customization, and content recommendation. Forecasting and analytics tools predict pipeline outcomes and analyze sales performance. AI improves forecast accuracy and identifies patterns that explain why some deals close and others don't. These tools inform strategy and resource allocation.

Virtual assistants and copilots provide general-purpose AI support across tasks. They can research prospects, draft communications, answer questions, and handle various activities that benefit from AI capability. Unlike specialized tools, assistants work across categories. Scheduling and automation tools handle administrative tasks like meeting coordination, data entry, and workflow triggering. AI enables smarter automation that adapts to context rather than following rigid rules. Each category addresses different aspects of sales work. Most organizations need capability across multiple categories, which raises questions about how tools work together.

Evaluating Individual Tools

Within each category, multiple vendors compete for attention. Evaluating which tool actually delivers on its promises requires looking beyond marketing claims. Capability verification separates genuine AI from marketing labels. Ask vendors to explain how their AI works. What data trains their models? What outcomes does their AI predict or optimize? How do they measure effectiveness? Vendors with real AI capability can answer these questions substantively. Vendors applying AI as a marketing term give vague responses. Relevance to your context determines whether general capability translates to your specific situation. A tool trained on inside sales data may not work for enterprise sales. A system optimized for technology markets may underperform in manufacturing. Ask about results for customers similar to you. Request references you can actually contact.

Data requirements clarify what the tool needs to function effectively. AI tools depend on data. If the tool requires data you don't have or can't provide, it won't perform as demonstrated. Understand exactly what data the tool needs and whether you can supply it. Integration capability determines how the tool connects with your existing stack. A standalone tool that doesn't integrate with your CRM, email system, and other platforms creates friction that reduces adoption. Ask specifically how the tool integrates with your current systems. Test the integrations before committing.

User experience affects whether salespeople will actually use the tool. The most capable AI doesn't help if it's too cumbersome to use. Evaluate how the tool fits into daily workflow. Will salespeople need to change how they work significantly? Is the interface intuitive? Does value delivery feel effortless or burdensome? Vendor stability matters because AI tools require ongoing development and support. A vendor that disappears or stops investing leaves you with capability that degrades over time. Evaluate the vendor's financial stability, customer base, and investment trajectory. Startups may offer innovative capability but carry higher risk. Established players offer stability but may innovate more slowly. Total cost extends beyond license fees.

Implementation takes time and money. Training requires investment. Ongoing management consumes resources. Integration maintenance has costs. Calculate the full cost, not just what appears on the invoice. These evaluation criteria apply across categories. Applying them systematically produces better tool decisions than relying on demos and sales pitches.

The Integration Challenge

Individual tools that work well in isolation can create problems in combination. The integration challenge is one of the most underestimated aspects of AI stack building. Data fragmentation occurs when different tools create separate data stores that don't communicate. Your conversation intelligence platform has data about calls. Your sales engagement platform has data about emails. Your CRM has data about opportunities. If these data sets don't integrate, you can't get unified views of customer interactions or AI analysis that considers all touchpoints. Workflow friction emerges when tools require separate logins, different interfaces, and manual data transfer between systems. Salespeople shouldn't need to copy information from one tool to another. They shouldn't need to switch between five applications to complete a single task. Workflow friction reduces adoption and erodes efficiency gains that AI was supposed to provide.

Conflicting recommendations can arise when multiple AI systems analyze the same situation and reach different conclusions. Your lead scoring tool says pursue this account. Your forecasting tool says it's unlikely to close. Your engagement platform suggests one approach while your conversation intelligence suggests another. Without integration that resolves conflicts, salespeople face confusion rather than clarity.

Maintenance burden compounds as the stack grows. Each integration requires monitoring. Updates to one system can break connections to others. Data mappings drift over time. The overhead of keeping everything working together can consume significant resources.

Security complexity increases with more tools accessing sensitive data. Each vendor with access to customer information represents a potential vulnerability. Each integration point is a potential security gap. Managing security across a complex stack requires attention that simpler architectures don't demand. These integration challenges don't mean you should avoid building a stack with multiple tools. They mean you should plan for integration deliberately, evaluate tools partly on how well they integrate, and budget for the ongoing work of maintaining connections.

Platform Versus Point Solution Strategy

A fundamental strategic choice shapes stack architecture: do you build around platforms that offer broad capability, or assemble best-of-breed point solutions for each function? Platform strategy anchors the stack on a comprehensive system that handles multiple categories. Major CRM vendors offer increasingly broad AI capability. All-in-one platforms promise unified data, consistent user experience, and reduced integration burden. The tradeoff is that platform capability in any single area may be less advanced than specialized point solutions.

Point solution strategy selects the best tool for each category regardless of vendor. This approach maximizes capability in each area but requires more integration work and creates more complex architecture. Managing multiple vendor relationships, separate contracts, and different update cycles adds overhead. Most organizations land somewhere between pure strategies. They anchor on a platform for core capability while adding point solutions for areas where specialized tools offer meaningfully better functionality. The question is which functions justify the complexity of point solutions and which are adequately served by platform capability.

Several factors inform this decision. How differentiated is the best point solution compared to platform alternatives? If the leading conversation intelligence tool is dramatically better than what your CRM platform offers, the complexity cost may be justified. If the difference is marginal, platform simplicity might outweigh capability edge. How critical is the function to your sales model? For capabilities central to your competitive advantage, accepting anything less than the best tool is costly. For peripheral functions, good enough from a platform may be truly good enough. How mature are your integration capabilities? Organizations with strong technical resources can manage complex stacks more easily. Organizations with limited technical capacity should bias toward platform consolidation.

Ian runs sales operations for a mid-sized software company. He evaluated whether to adopt a specialized forecasting tool or use the forecasting features in their existing CRM platform. The specialized tool demonstrated meaningfully better accuracy in their evaluation, but integration proved difficult. Forecast data didn't flow cleanly into reports built on CRM data. Salespeople had to check two systems to understand pipeline status. After six months, he migrated to platform forecasting. The accuracy was somewhat lower, but the unified view and simpler workflow produced better actual outcomes.

Data Considerations

AI tools are only as good as the data they access. Data strategy should precede tool selection rather than following it. Data availability determines what AI capabilities are possible. Conversation intelligence requires call recordings. Engagement optimization requires communication history. Predictive scoring requires historical outcome data. Before evaluating tools, inventory what data you have and what you can realistically capture. Data quality affects AI performance directly. Models trained on accurate data produce useful predictions. Models trained on messy data produce garbage. CRM records with inconsistent entry, outdated information, and missing fields undermine AI tools that depend on them. Investment in data quality often produces better return than investment in more sophisticated tools.

Data unification enables AI that works across information sources. Customer interactions span calls, emails, meetings, website visits, and more. AI that sees all these touchpoints produces better insights than AI limited to one channel. Unifying data from disparate sources is challenging but valuable. Data access governance controls what tools can see and do with information. Customer data may be subject to privacy regulations. Competitive information may be confidential. Internal data may require access restrictions. AI tools need access to function, but access should be appropriate to the tool's purpose and vendor's trustworthiness. Data portability affects flexibility. If your AI tools depend on data trapped in proprietary formats, switching tools becomes expensive. Data strategies that maintain portability preserve options for the future. Organizations that neglect data considerations often find themselves unable to use AI tools they've purchased. The tools sit idle because data isn't available, isn't clean enough, or isn't accessible. Data investment is prerequisite to AI capability, not optional complement.

Build Versus Buy Decisions

Organizations with technical resources face choices between building custom AI capability and buying commercial tools. The decision involves tradeoffs that vary by situation. Buy advantages include faster deployment, proven capability, vendor-supported maintenance, and access to innovation without internal investment. Commercial tools embody accumulated learning from many customers. They're designed for usability by non-technical salespeople. Updates happen without your development resources. Build advantages include customization to your specific needs, integration with your specific systems, and control over capability direction. Custom development can address requirements that commercial tools don't serve. Proprietary AI capability can provide competitive differentiation that shared tools can't.

Hybrid approaches combine commercial foundation with custom extensions. You might use a commercial CRM and conversation intelligence platform while building custom analytics that address your specific business questions. The hybrid approach captures benefits of both while managing complexity. The decision depends on your resources, your requirements, and how differentiated your needs are from what commercial tools serve. Organizations with unique sales models, unusual data assets, or specific analytical requirements find more value in custom development. Organizations with more standard needs typically find commercial tools more efficient.

Several questions guide the build-versus-buy analysis. Is there a commercial tool that addresses your requirement adequately? If yes, building custom solution is hard to justify unless strategic differentiation demands it. Do you have the technical resources to build and maintain custom capability? Building without adequate resources produces abandoned projects. Is the capability core to competitive advantage or supporting infrastructure? Core capabilities may warrant custom investment. Infrastructure is usually better purchased.

Pilot Programs and Proof of Concept

Effective evaluation requires more than vendor demos. Pilot programs that test tools on actual work reveal realities that controlled demonstrations hide. Pilot design should include clear success criteria defined before the pilot begins. What outcomes would convince you the tool works? What metrics will you measure? Without predefined criteria, pilots become opinion exercises where results are interpreted to confirm existing biases. Representative conditions mean testing with typical users on typical work. A pilot conducted by your most technically sophisticated salespeople on your easiest opportunities doesn't predict how the tool will perform broadly. Include average performers and difficult situations.

Adequate duration allows initial learning curves to pass and sustainable patterns to emerge. Tools often perform well in the first week of enthusiastic attention, then decline as novelty fades. Pilots should run long enough to reach steady state, typically at least one quarter. Control comparison enables attribution of results to the tool rather than other factors. If possible, compare piloted users to similar users without the tool. Without comparison, you can't know whether observed results came from the tool or from other causes.

Cost tracking during pilots captures actual implementation effort, not just license fees. How much time did setup require? What problems emerged that required resolution? How much training was needed? These costs inform full rollout planning. User feedback reveals adoption barriers that metrics might miss. Do salespeople find the tool useful? What frustrates them? What would they change? Feedback helps predict whether adoption will sustain beyond the pilot period. Pilots that follow these principles produce reliable insight about whether tools will deliver value at scale. Pilots that skip them produce decisions based on incomplete information.

Total Cost of Ownership

The true cost of AI tools exceeds what appears on the invoice. Understanding total cost prevents budget surprises and enables meaningful comparison between alternatives. License and subscription fees are the visible starting point. Understand pricing models: per user, per use, per feature tier. Understand how pricing scales as usage grows. Understand what happens when contracts renew. Implementation costs include setup, configuration, data migration, and integration development. Some tools implement in hours. Others require months of project work. Implementation cost varies enormously and can exceed first-year license fees for complex tools.

Training costs include both direct expense and opportunity cost of time spent learning rather than selling. How much training does the tool require? Who delivers it? How long before users achieve proficiency? Ongoing training for new hires and feature updates adds recurring cost. Integration maintenance requires ongoing attention as connected systems update and change. Budget for technical resources to monitor and maintain integrations. Budget for troubleshooting when things break.

Administration overhead covers user management, configuration updates, and vendor relationship management. More tools mean more administration. Complex tools require more administration than simple ones. Opportunity cost is the value of alternatives forgone. Money spent on one tool isn't available for others. Time spent implementing one capability isn't available for other priorities. Consider what you're not doing because you're doing this. Exit costs materialize when you eventually move to something else. How difficult is it to extract your data? What processes depend on the tool that will need rebuilding? High exit costs create lock-in that reduces future flexibility. Calculating total cost requires estimating these components honestly. Vendors naturally emphasize low sticker prices while downplaying implementation complexity and ongoing overhead. Your job is understanding actual cost, not believing convenient estimates.

Procurement and Vendor Management

How you buy affects what you get and what you pay. Procurement approaches can create value or destroy it. Competitive evaluation creates leverage. Vendors competing for your business offer better pricing and terms than vendors who know they're the only option. Even if you have a preferred choice, evaluate alternatives to inform negotiation. Pilot-to-purchase pathways establish expectations about what happens after successful pilots. Don't pilot without understanding what procurement looks like if the pilot succeeds. Avoid situations where successful pilots lead to difficult negotiations because procurement wasn't prepared.

Contract terms deserve attention beyond pricing. What happens if the tool doesn't perform as expected? What service level commitments exist? What are the terms for data access and portability? How do renewals work? Contract terms that seem minor at signing can become significant later. Vendor relationship affects ongoing experience. Your account manager's responsiveness, the vendor's investment in customer success, and the quality of support all matter. Reference checks should explore relationship quality, not just tool capability.

Multi-year considerations inform structure. Longer commitments typically secure better pricing but reduce flexibility. Shorter commitments preserve options but may cost more annually. The right term depends on confidence in the tool and expectation of market changes. Stakeholder alignment ensures that everyone affected by the purchase agrees on requirements and decision criteria. Purchases that surprise stakeholders create implementation challenges and relationship damage regardless of tool quality.

Evolving the Stack Over Time

Stack building isn't a one-time project. It's an ongoing process of evolution as needs change and market offerings improve. Regular capability review assesses whether current tools still meet requirements. The tool that was best available three years ago may no longer be competitive. Requirements that were met adequately may have grown. Periodic review identifies gaps and opportunities. Sunset planning prepares for tool replacement before it becomes urgent. Every tool will eventually be replaced. Knowing when and how to exit current tools enables smoother transitions than emergency replacements.

Market monitoring tracks what's becoming available. New tools emerge. Existing tools add capability. Understanding market evolution informs both current optimization and future planning. Experimentation tests new capabilities on limited scope before broad adoption. Innovation often comes from smaller vendors whose tools can be tested without major commitment. A culture of experimentation discovers opportunities that pure maintenance misses. Documentation captures what you have, how it's configured, and why decisions were made. Stacks that exist only in people's heads become fragile as people leave. Documented architecture enables maintenance and evolution. The stack that's right today won't be right forever. Building with evolution in mind produces architectures that adapt rather than calcify.

Making the Decision

Stack decisions ultimately require judgment that balances competing considerations. Frameworks help structure thinking, but judgment determines conclusions. The decision process should start with clear requirements. What capabilities do you need? What problems are you solving? Requirements should come from understanding sales process needs, not from vendor feature lists.

Evaluation should follow the principles outlined in this chapter: verify capability, confirm relevance to your context, assess integration, understand costs, and pilot before committing. Decisions should involve appropriate stakeholders. Sales leadership understands requirements. IT understands integration and maintenance. Finance understands cost. Procurement understands vendor management. Cross-functional input produces better decisions.

Timing matters. Don't rush decisions that lock you in for years. Don't delay decisions that prevent capability development while you optimize endlessly. Find the balance between due diligence and action. Finally, recognize that perfect decisions are impossible. You can't know everything. The market will change. Your needs will evolve. Make the best decision you can with available information, then be prepared to adapt as you learn more.

Beyond the Stack

Building an AI sales stack is necessary but not sufficient for AI success. Tools provide capability. Using them well produces results. The question after stack building is whether the investment delivers expected return. How do you know if AI tools are actually helping? How do you measure their contribution? How do you optimize their use based on what the data shows?

The next chapter addresses measuring AI impact. It provides frameworks for establishing baselines, tracking outcomes, and calculating return on investment. Measurement creates accountability for AI investments and provides feedback for continuous improvement. Leaders who can demonstrate AI ROI make better decisions and secure resources for further capability building.

Chapter Thirteen

Measuring AI Impact

The Accountability Imperative

AI investments consume resources. Licenses cost money. Implementation takes time. Training diverts attention from selling. Ongoing management requires effort. These investments deserve scrutiny. Are they producing returns that justify the cost? Many organizations can't answer this question. They adopted AI tools because competitors did, because vendors promised results, or because leadership declared AI a priority. The tools are in place. People are using them. But nobody knows with certainty whether the investment is paying off. This measurement gap creates problems. Without evidence of impact, AI investments become vulnerable when budgets tighten. Without feedback on what's working, optimization is impossible. Without demonstrated ROI, the case for further investment relies on faith rather than data.

Measuring AI impact is difficult. Multiple factors affect sales results. Isolating AI's contribution from other influences requires careful methodology. But difficult doesn't mean impossible. Organizations that approach measurement systematically develop understanding that guides better decisions and justifies continued investment. This chapter provides frameworks for measuring AI impact on sales performance. The goal isn't academic precision. It's practical insight that enables accountability, optimization, and informed decision-making.

Defining What to Measure

Measurement starts with clarity about what success looks like. Different AI tools serve different purposes and require different metrics. Efficiency metrics capture time savings and productivity improvements. If an AI tool is supposed to reduce administrative burden, measure how much time salespeople spend on administration before and after. If it's supposed to accelerate research, measure research time. Efficiency metrics answer whether AI is making work faster. Activity metrics track volume of sales activities: calls made, emails sent, meetings held, proposals generated. These metrics matter when AI is supposed to enable salespeople to do more. They're insufficient alone because activity without effectiveness wastes time, but they indicate whether efficiency gains are being reinvested in sales activity.

Quality metrics assess how well activities are performed. Call scores, response rates, engagement levels, and customer satisfaction ratings all fall into this category. These metrics matter when AI is supposed to improve how well things are done, not just how much gets done. A conversation intelligence tool should improve call quality. A personalization tool should improve response rates. Outcome metrics measure actual business results: revenue, conversion rates, deal size, win rates, and quota attainment. These metrics are the ultimate test of whether AI investment translates to business value. But they're also the hardest to attribute to specific tools because many factors influence outcomes.

Leading indicators predict future results before they materialize. Pipeline velocity, engagement trends, and leading activity patterns enable earlier feedback than waiting for closed deals. If AI improves leading indicators, outcome improvements should follow. Lagging indicators confirm results after the fact. Annual revenue, customer lifetime value, and market share provide ultimate validation but arrive too late to guide near-term decisions. Most AI measurement approaches combine metrics across categories. Efficiency and activity metrics provide early feedback. Quality metrics connect activities to effectiveness. Outcome metrics validate business impact. Leading indicators enable optimization. Lagging indicators confirm long-term value.

Establishing Baselines

Measurement requires comparison. Impact is the difference between what happened with AI and what would have happened without it. Without baselines, this comparison is impossible. Pre-implementation baselines capture performance before AI tools are deployed. If you want to know whether AI improved conversion rates, you need to know what conversion rates were before. If you want to know whether AI saved time, you need to know how time was spent before. Baseline data should be collected with the same rigor you'll apply to post-implementation measurement. Concurrent control groups provide comparison during implementation. Some salespeople or teams use AI tools while others don't. The difference in results between groups indicates AI impact. Control groups work well when you can create comparable populations and maintain the control condition long enough to measure meaningful outcomes.

Historical comparison uses past performance as baseline. This approach works when control groups aren't feasible, but it's vulnerable to confounding factors. If the market was different, if the product changed, if the team composition shifted, then differences from historical baselines may not reflect AI impact. Counterfactual estimation attempts to model what would have happened without AI. Statistical techniques can estimate this counterfactual using historical patterns and external factors. The approach is more sophisticated than simple before-after comparison but requires analytical capability and makes assumptions that affect conclusions. Baseline choice affects what conclusions you can draw. Weak baselines produce weak evidence. Strong baselines enable confident attribution. The right baseline approach depends on your situation, but establishing some baseline is essential. Without it, you're measuring activity, not impact.

Isolating AI Contribution

Sales results depend on many factors beyond AI tools. Market conditions, competitive dynamics, product changes, pricing, marketing activity, individual salesperson capability, and luck all influence outcomes. Isolating AI's contribution from these other factors is the central challenge of AI measurement. Several approaches help with isolation. Controlled experiments randomly assign salespeople or accounts to treatment and control groups. Random assignment ensures that groups are comparable on factors other than AI use. Differences in outcomes can be attributed to AI with reasonable confidence. This approach is the gold standard but isn't always practical. You may not be able to withhold tools from some salespeople. Market conditions may not allow clean experiments. Matched comparison pairs similar salespeople or accounts, with one using AI and one not. Matching on characteristics like experience, territory, and historical performance controls for known differences. The approach is weaker than random assignment because it can't control for unmeasured differences, but it's often more practical.

Time-series analysis examines performance trends over time, looking for changes that coincide with AI implementation. If conversion rates were flat for years and then increased when AI tools launched, the timing suggests attribution. The approach is vulnerable to other changes that happened simultaneously, but it provides evidence when controlled comparison isn't possible. Regression analysis statistically models the relationship between AI use and outcomes while controlling for other measured factors. If higher AI tool usage correlates with better results after controlling for experience, territory, and market conditions, the relationship suggests impact. The approach requires analytical sophistication and can only control for factors that are measured. Natural experiments exploit situations where AI access varied for reasons unrelated to expected performance. A system outage that affected some regions but not others. A staged rollout that reached some teams before others. These accidental variations create comparison opportunities that weren't designed but can be analyzed. Perfect isolation is impossible. There will always be unmeasured factors that could explain differences. The goal isn't certainty but reasonable confidence. Multiple approaches pointing to the same conclusion provide stronger evidence than any single analysis.

Common Measurement Pitfalls

Measurement mistakes lead to wrong conclusions and bad decisions. Several pitfalls are common enough to warrant explicit attention. Confusing correlation with causation is the most pervasive pitfall. Salespeople who use AI tools heavily may perform better, but that doesn't prove AI caused the better performance. Maybe high performers are more likely to adopt new tools. Maybe certain territories lend themselves to both AI use and better results. Correlation establishes association. Causation requires ruling out alternative explanations. Measuring activity instead of outcomes produces misleading comfort. High AI tool usage feels like success. Many calls made with AI assistance feels like progress. But if activity doesn't translate to results, the measurement is tracking effort, not impact. Activity metrics should connect to outcome metrics or they don't demonstrate business value.

Selection bias distorts conclusions when AI users differ systematically from non-users. Pilots often include the most enthusiastic, capable salespeople. These people would outperform anyway. Attributing their success to AI overstates the tool's contribution. Measurement designs should account for who chooses or is chosen to use AI. Survivorship bias ignores failures. If you only measure salespeople who continued using AI tools, you miss those who tried and abandoned them. The remaining users may show positive results while the overall investment was negative because many people tried and failed.

Regression to the mean explains apparent improvement that isn't real. If you implement AI when performance is unusually low, performance will likely improve simply by returning to normal. If you measure the best-performing users of a new tool, their next period will likely be worse simply because extreme performance doesn't persist. These statistical effects masquerade as tool impact. Cherry-picking time periods allows finding whatever conclusion you want. Performance varies. If you measure the best quarter after AI implementation and compare it to an average quarter before, you'll find improvement that reflects variability rather than impact. Measurement should use consistent, predetermined time periods. Ignoring costs makes any positive outcome look like success. If AI tools produce ten percent more revenue but cost more than that revenue increase, the investment isn't paying off. ROI requires considering both returns and investment.

Felix leads revenue operations and was asked to demonstrate AI tool impact to the executive team. His initial analysis showed that salespeople who used the conversation intelligence platform closed deals at higher rates. But when he dug deeper, he discovered that the platform was primarily used by senior salespeople who had always closed at higher rates. The correlation reflected experience, not tool impact. He redesigned the analysis to compare salespeople with similar experience and tenure. The tool impact was still positive but much smaller than the initial analysis suggested. His honest reporting built credibility even though it tempered enthusiasm about the tool.

Calculating Return on Investment

ROI quantifies whether AI investment is worthwhile. The basic formula is simple: (Return - Investment) / Investment. Application to AI is more complex because both return and investment require careful calculation. Return calculation estimates the value AI created. For efficiency gains, this means estimating the value of time saved. If AI saves each salesperson five hours weekly, what's that time worth? If that time goes to selling activities that produce pipeline, what's the revenue impact? These calculations require assumptions, but explicit assumptions are better than implicit ones. For quality improvements, return means the value of better outcomes. Higher conversion rates produce more closed deals from the same pipeline. Better customer satisfaction produces higher retention and expansion. Quantify these improvements in revenue or profit impact. For new capability, return means business enabled that wouldn't have happened otherwise. Deals won because AI-enabled personalization differentiated your approach. Markets entered because AI made them addressable. These returns can be substantial but are harder to quantify.

Investment calculation should capture total cost of ownership, not just license fees. Include implementation costs, training time, ongoing management, integration maintenance, and opportunity cost. Use actual costs where known and estimates where necessary. Understating investment overstates ROI. Time horizon affects ROI conclusions. Short-term calculations may miss benefits that take time to materialize. Long-term calculations involve more uncertainty about future returns. Most organizations calculate ROI over one to three years, recognizing that shorter periods may be misleading and longer periods involve too much uncertainty.

Risk adjustment acknowledges that projected returns may not materialize. A tool that reliably produces modest returns may be a better investment than one that might produce large returns but carries significant uncertainty. Risk-adjusted ROI discounts uncertain returns appropriately. Comparison to alternatives puts ROI in context. An AI tool with 50% ROI sounds good until you discover that the same investment in hiring more salespeople would produce 80% ROI. ROI matters relative to other uses of the same resources.

Building Feedback Loops

Measurement should drive action. The point isn't just knowing whether AI works. It's using that knowledge to improve. Performance dashboards make AI impact visible on an ongoing basis. Rather than periodic analyses, continuous monitoring shows trends as they develop. Dashboards should show both leading indicators for early warning and outcome metrics for validation. They should highlight variances from expectations that warrant investigation. Usage analytics track how AI tools are actually being used. Which features get adopted? Which are ignored? Where do people struggle? Usage data identifies adoption barriers and optimization opportunities. Tools that aren't being used can't produce results. Understanding why enables intervention.

Outcome linkage connects specific AI applications to specific results. Which AI-assisted approaches produce better outcomes? Which produce worse? This linkage enables optimization of how AI is used, not just whether it's used. Maybe AI email drafts work well for prospecting but poorly for renewal conversations. Outcome linkage surfaces these patterns. User feedback captures qualitative insight that quantitative metrics miss. What do salespeople find helpful? What frustrates them? What would they change? Regular feedback collection reveals improvement opportunities that numbers alone don't show.

Iteration cycles use measurement findings to drive changes. Monthly or quarterly reviews should examine what the data shows, what hypotheses it suggests, and what changes to test. These cycles make measurement actionable rather than just informational. The feedback loop should be explicit: measure, analyze, hypothesize, change, measure again. Without this discipline, measurement becomes a reporting exercise rather than an improvement engine.

Communicating Impact to Stakeholders

Demonstrating AI impact to stakeholders requires translation from analytical findings to business language. Different audiences need different presentations. Executive leadership cares about business impact and strategic implications. Lead with revenue and profit effects. Connect AI impact to strategic priorities. Show ROI in terms leadership uses for other investments. Executives don't need methodological details. They need confidence that conclusions are valid and implications are clear. Finance cares about cost justification and resource allocation. Provide detailed cost accounting. Show how returns were calculated. Enable comparison to other investment alternatives. Finance needs to trust the numbers, which means transparency about assumptions and methodology.

Sales leadership cares about team performance and capability development. Show how AI affects quota attainment and sales metrics. Highlight which practices produce best results. Provide guidance for coaching and development. Sales leaders need operational implications they can act on. IT and operations care about technical performance and resource requirements. Provide system metrics alongside business metrics. Show adoption rates and usage patterns. Identify technical issues affecting impact. These stakeholders enable AI success and need relevant information. Salespeople themselves care about how AI helps them individually. Show personal productivity gains. Provide individual performance data where appropriate. Explain how measurement informs decisions that affect them. Buy-in from users depends on their believing that AI and its measurement serve their interests. Effective communication adapts the same core findings to each audience. The underlying analysis is the same. The presentation varies by what each audience needs to understand and believe.

Measurement Maturity Progression

Organizations develop measurement capability over time. Understanding where you are on this progression helps identify appropriate next steps. Stage one involves activity tracking, measuring whether AI tools are being used. Login rates, feature usage, and engagement metrics confirm adoption but don't demonstrate impact. Most organizations start here because the data is readily available. Stage two moves to output measurement, tracking what AI-assisted activities produce. Calls made, emails sent, proposals generated. This stage connects tool use to sales activity but doesn't demonstrate that activity translates to results.

Stage three advances to outcome correlation, examining relationships between AI use and business results. Do high AI users perform better? Does AI-assisted prospecting produce more pipeline? This stage provides suggestive evidence but can't establish causation. Stage four involves causal analysis, attempting to isolate AI's contribution using controlled comparisons, statistical techniques, or natural experiments. This stage provides stronger evidence but requires more analytical sophistication. Stage five represents optimization, using measurement to drive continuous improvement. Feedback loops refine AI application.

A/B testing identifies best practices. Measurement enables action, not just reporting. This stage extracts maximum value from measurement investment. Most organizations should aim to reach at least stage three quickly and stage four over time. Stage five represents mature capability that few organizations achieve but all should aspire to.

When Measurement Shows Problems

Measurement sometimes reveals that AI isn't working as expected. These findings are valuable even when they're unwelcome. Low adoption means tools aren't being used enough to produce impact. Measurement can identify who isn't adopting, what barriers exist, and where intervention is needed. Low adoption isn't AI failure. It's implementation failure that measurement helps diagnose. Neutral impact means AI isn't producing measurable improvement. This finding should prompt investigation. Is the tool being used correctly? Are expectations realistic? Is the measurement methodology sound? Neutral impact might reflect bad tools, bad implementation, or bad measurement.

Negative impact means AI is making things worse. This can happen. AI recommendations might be wrong for your context. Automation might be damaging customer relationships. Efficiency gains might be coming at quality cost. Negative findings should stop harmful practices, not be dismissed or hidden. Inconsistent impact means AI works for some situations but not others. This finding guides optimization. Double down on applications that work. Fix or abandon applications that don't. Inconsistency is information that enables smarter AI deployment. The value of measurement comes from honest engagement with findings, including uncomfortable ones. Organizations that only accept positive findings and explain away negative ones don't actually benefit from measurement. They're just going through motions.

The Measurement Investment

Measurement itself requires investment. Data infrastructure, analytical capability, time for analysis, and attention for review all cost something. This investment needs justification too. The case for measurement investment rests on better decisions. Without measurement, AI investments are bets based on vendor promises and competitor behavior. With measurement, decisions rest on evidence about what actually works in your context.

The investment scales with the stakes. A small AI tool investment might warrant only basic activity tracking. A major platform commitment deserves rigorous impact analysis. Measurement investment should be proportional to the decisions it informs. The investment also pays off through optimization. Measurement that drives continuous improvement produces compounding returns. The feedback loops enabled by measurement make AI investments more effective over time.

Carmela runs sales enablement for a financial services firm. She allocated significant budget to AI tools based on industry hype and executive enthusiasm. When results disappointed, she couldn't explain why or what to do differently. She then invested in measurement capability: better data tracking, analytical resources, and regular review processes. The next round of AI investments was smaller but more targeted, based on what measurement showed was working. Results improved. The measurement investment paid for itself through better AI investment decisions.

From Measurement to Responsibility

Measurement demonstrates what AI does. It shows where AI helps and where it doesn't. It quantifies costs and benefits. It enables accountability for investments. But measurement doesn't tell you whether what AI does is right. A tool might demonstrate positive ROI while raising ethical concerns. An application might improve metrics while damaging trust. Measurement captures impact but not propriety.

The question of what AI should do, not just what it can do, requires different frameworks. Ethical considerations, customer welfare, long-term relationship health, and organizational values all matter beyond what measurement captures. The next chapter examines ethics and responsibility in AI-powered sales. It addresses the questions that measurement can't answer: When is AI use appropriate? What limits should apply? How do you make ethical decisions when guidelines are unclear? These questions become more pressing as AI capability grows and as measurement demonstrates that AI works, raising the stakes for ensuring it's used responsibly.

Chapter Fourteen

Ethics and Responsibility in AI-Powered Sales

Why Ethics Demands Attention

AI expands what salespeople can do. It enables deeper customer surveillance, more sophisticated manipulation, and wider reach than ever before. These capabilities can be used well or poorly. The choice between them is an ethical choice that every sales professional and organization must make. The temptation to dismiss ethics as abstract philosophy misunderstands its practical importance. Ethical violations erode trust. Eroded trust undermines sales effectiveness. The salesperson who gains short-term advantage through ethically questionable AI use often pays long-term costs that exceed the gains. Ethics isn't just about being good. It's about being smart. The most successful long-term sales professionals understand that how you win matters as much as whether you win.

But ethics is also about being good, and that matters independently of strategic calculation. Sales professionals are people with values. Most want to feel proud of how they work. Most don't want to succeed through manipulation or deception. The question of how to use AI ethically matters because it affects what kind of professional you become and what kind of work you can be proud of. When you look back on your career, the deals won through questionable means won't feel like victories.

This chapter examines ethical dimensions of AI in sales comprehensively. It doesn't provide simple rules for every situation. Ethical questions rarely have simple answers. Instead, it provides frameworks for thinking through challenges, principles for guiding decisions, and perspective on why ethical practice serves both moral and practical interests. The goal is to equip you with the thinking tools needed to navigate situations where the right path isn't obvious.

Privacy and Customer Data

AI's power comes from data. The more data available about customers, the more effectively AI can target, personalize, and predict. This creates pressure to gather as much data as possible and use it as extensively as possible. Privacy concerns push back against this pressure, creating tension that every AI-enabled sales organization must navigate.

Privacy matters because customers have legitimate interests in controlling information about themselves. They may not want their browsing behavior tracked. They may not want their communications analyzed. They may not want their personal characteristics used to target them.

These preferences deserve respect regardless of whether data use is technically legal. The fact that you can collect and use certain data doesn't mean you should.

The legal landscape provides floor rather than ceiling. Regulations like GDPR and various privacy laws establish minimum requirements. But legal compliance doesn't equal ethical conduct. Practices can be legal while still violating reasonable customer expectations about how their information is used. A customer who learns that their data was used in ways they never imagined, even if those uses were technically permitted by terms of service they clicked through without reading, will feel violated regardless of legal technicalities.

Several questions help assess whether data practices are ethically sound. Start by asking whether customers meaningfully consented. Burying data permissions in lengthy terms of service that nobody reads doesn't constitute meaningful consent. If customers would be surprised to learn how their data is being used, consent is probably insufficient. Ethical practice involves clear disclosure and genuine choice, not legal cover disguised as consent.

Consider whether data use is proportional to customer benefit. Using extensive personal data to provide better, more relevant service represents a value exchange customers might accept. Using the same data purely to maximize sales pressure without customer benefit is harder to justify. The extent of data use should correlate with customer value received. If you're gathering data primarily to serve your interests rather than theirs, that imbalance warrants scrutiny.

Ask whether data is being combined in ways customers wouldn't expect. Combining data from multiple sources can reveal information that no single source provides. A customer's purchase history combined with their social media activity combined with their location data creates a profile more invasive than any single input. Such combination requires particular scrutiny because the whole reveals more than the sum of its parts.

Examine how secure customer data is. Collecting data creates responsibility for protecting it. Data breaches harm customers regardless of how ethically the data was collected. Security investment should match the sensitivity of data held. An organization that gathers extensive customer data but underinvests in security is making an ethical choice, even if they don't frame it that way.

Finally, consider what happens when relationships end. Customers who leave should be able to have their data deleted or restricted. Retaining and continuing to use data from former customers raises ethical concerns, especially if they weren't informed this would happen. The relationship has ended, but the data lives on, sometimes in ways the customer never anticipated. These questions don't produce automatic answers. They require judgment applied to specific situations. But asking them systematically helps identify practices that warrant reconsideration. Organizations that never ask these questions will eventually face situations where they wish they had.

Fairness in AI Applications

AI systems can perpetuate and amplify unfairness in ways that aren't immediately visible. Algorithms trained on historical data may encode historical biases. Optimization for efficiency may disadvantage certain groups. The apparent objectivity of algorithmic decisions can mask underlying inequity, making unfairness harder to detect and challenge than when humans made the same decisions explicitly.

Lead scoring fairness deserves particular attention. If a scoring model was trained on historical data about which leads converted, and historical conversion patterns reflected biased practices, the model will perpetuate those biases. A model that downscores leads from certain geographic areas, company types, or buyer characteristics may be encoding unfairness rather than genuine fit assessment. The algorithm seems objective, but it's learning from a history that wasn't. Pricing algorithm fairness raises concerns when AI enables differential pricing based on customer characteristics. Charging higher prices to customers identified as less price-sensitive might maximize revenue but may also correlate with demographic characteristics in problematic ways. Dynamic pricing that systematically disadvantages certain customer groups warrants ethical scrutiny, even when no one intended discriminatory outcomes.

Opportunity allocation fairness matters when AI influences which salespeople receive which leads or territories. If allocation algorithms favor certain salespeople in ways that correlate with protected characteristics, the system creates unfair competitive dynamics within the sales organization. The salespeople disadvantaged by these algorithms may never know why their opportunities seem worse than their colleagues'. Communication fairness applies to AI-generated content. Do AI messaging systems communicate differently to different groups in ways that could be discriminatory? Does personalization cross into differential treatment that disadvantages certain customers? These questions require examination because AI systems don't announce when they're treating people differently in problematic ways.

Detecting unfairness requires actively looking for it. AI systems don't flag their own biased outcomes. Organizations must audit their AI applications for fairness, examining whether outcomes differ across groups and whether those differences are justifiable. This auditing isn't optional if you care about fairness. It's the only way to know whether your systems are behaving ethically. When unfairness is discovered, the response shouldn't be simply turning off the AI. The question is whether the unfair outcome reflects AI amplifying problems or AI revealing problems that existed in human practice too. Sometimes fixing the AI also fixes human processes. Sometimes AI provides the visibility needed to address issues that were always present but hidden. Either way, discovery is an opportunity for improvement, not just a problem to eliminate.

Transparency in Automated Interactions

Customers increasingly interact with AI without knowing it. Chatbots handle inquiries. AI generates emails that appear to come from humans. Automated systems make decisions about which customers receive which offers. The question of how transparent to be about AI involvement has ethical dimensions that deserve careful thought. Active deception is clearly wrong. If a customer directly asks whether they're communicating with a human and receives a false answer, that's straightforward deception. No efficiency gain or competitive advantage justifies lying to customers about who or what they're interacting with. This line is bright and shouldn't be crossed.

Passive non-disclosure is more complicated. Does every AI-assisted email require an "AI wrote this" disclaimer? Probably not, any more than every email requires disclosure of what software generated it. But when AI involvement would materially affect customer perception of the interaction, non-disclosure becomes problematic. The question is whether customers would care if they knew. The reasonable expectation test helps navigate this ambiguity. Would a reasonable customer expect to know about AI involvement in this context? If a customer believes they're receiving personal attention from a salesperson who knows them, when actually they're receiving AI-generated content based on data analysis, the gap between expectation and reality matters. Practices that depend on customers not knowing the truth are ethically suspect, even when no explicit lies are told.

Context affects expectations significantly. In some contexts, customers assume AI involvement and don't expect otherwise. Automated scheduling, chatbot support for basic questions, and algorithmic product recommendations don't typically surprise customers. In other contexts, like complex negotiations or sensitive communications, customers expect human engagement and would feel deceived to learn otherwise. Understanding what customers expect in each context guides appropriate transparency.

Transparency isn't only about disclosure. It's about not creating false impressions through strategic omission. The salesperson who carefully avoids mentioning AI involvement while cultivating an impression of personal attention may never technically lie while still deceiving. The absence of lies doesn't guarantee the presence of honesty. Ethical practice requires considering the impressions you create, not just the statements you make.

Accountability for AI Mistakes

AI systems make mistakes. They misidentify prospects, generate inappropriate content, make wrong predictions, and sometimes cause harm. When things go wrong, accountability questions arise that don't have easy answers. Organizational accountability is clear in principle. The organization that deploys AI is responsible for what it does. "The algorithm did it" is not a defense. Organizations choose which AI to deploy, how to configure it, and where to apply it. They bear responsibility for outcomes even when AI intermediates between decision and result. This responsibility can't be delegated to vendors or attributed to technology.

Individual accountability is more complex. A salesperson who acts on AI recommendations that turn out to be wrong may feel they were just following the system. But salespeople retain responsibility for their actions. If an AI recommendation seemed obviously wrong and the salesperson followed it anyway, they bear responsibility for that choice. They had the opportunity to exercise judgment and didn't. If the recommendation seemed reasonable and they had no way to know it was wrong, accountability shifts toward those who created or deployed the AI. The key question is whether the individual had reasonable opportunity to catch the error.

Vendor accountability matters in tool selection. If you purchase AI tools that prove unreliable or harmful, you're responsible for what you do with them. But vendors who misrepresent capabilities or conceal known problems bear their own accountability. Evaluation should consider vendor accountability track record. Have they been honest about limitations? Have they responded appropriately when problems emerged? These questions inform whether a vendor deserves your trust and your business.

Error correction is an accountability obligation that extends beyond fixing immediate problems. When AI mistakes cause harm, accountability requires understanding what went wrong, preventing recurrence, and making affected parties whole where possible. Simply apologizing and moving on isn't sufficient when systemic issues caused the problem.

Nadine manages accounts in the healthcare sector. An AI-generated proposal included a pricing error that significantly underquoted a complex implementation. The customer accepted, and honoring the quote would cost her company substantial margin. The AI had been configured incorrectly, but she had signed the proposal without verifying the numbers. Accountability was shared: the organization for the configuration error, Nadine for failing to verify, and the process for lacking adequate controls. The resolution involved honoring the quote while implementing verification steps to prevent recurrence. Accountability meant accepting consequences and improving practices, not assigning blame and moving on. Everyone involved learned something about their responsibilities.

The Manipulation Question

AI enables sophisticated influence techniques. Personalization can become manipulation when it exploits psychological vulnerabilities. Timing optimization can become pressure when it targets moments of weakness. The line between persuasion and manipulation deserves careful consideration because AI makes crossing that line easier than ever.

Persuasion respects customer autonomy. It provides information, makes arguments, and presents options. The customer remains in control of their decision. They have access to relevant facts and can evaluate them according to their own interests. Persuasion treats customers as rational agents capable of making their own choices. Manipulation undermines autonomy. It exploits cognitive biases, creates false urgency, withholds material information, or otherwise leads customers to decisions they wouldn't make with full information and clear thinking. The customer is treated as a target to be moved rather than a person to be served. Manipulation succeeds by circumventing rather than engaging the customer's judgment.

AI makes manipulation easier and more tempting. Systems that analyze customer psychology can identify vulnerabilities. Systems that optimize timing can target moments when resistance is lowest. Systems that personalize content can craft messages that push specific psychological buttons. The capability exists and keeps expanding. The question is whether to use it. The ethical principle is clear: don't manipulate. But application requires judgment because the line between persuasion and manipulation isn't always obvious. Several factors indicate when persuasion has crossed into manipulation.

Exploiting known vulnerabilities crosses the line. If you know a customer makes poor decisions under time pressure and deliberately create artificial urgency, that's manipulation. If you know someone responds to fear appeals and craft messaging to trigger anxiety, that's manipulation. You're using knowledge of their weaknesses against them rather than helping them make good decisions. Withholding material information crosses the line. Persuasion can emphasize positive features. Manipulation conceals relevant drawbacks. If your solution has significant limitations that would affect the customer's decision, ethical practice requires disclosure even if it hurts the sale. The customer deserves to make an informed choice, not one based on incomplete information you strategically withheld.

Creating false impressions crosses the line. Personalization that makes customers believe they're receiving individual attention they're not actually getting manipulates their perception of the relationship. Testimonials or social proof that are fabricated or misleading manipulate trust. These practices may not involve explicit lies, but they create beliefs in customers that don't reflect reality. Targeting impaired decision-making crosses the line. Customers experiencing stress, fatigue, or cognitive overload are more susceptible to influence. Ethical practice avoids exploiting these states even when they can be detected and targeted. The fact that you can identify when someone is vulnerable doesn't give you license to take advantage of that vulnerability.

Competitive Pressure and Ethical Constraints

Ethics would be simpler if competitors were also ethical. In reality, some competitors will use AI in ways you've decided are wrong. They'll gather more data, manipulate more aggressively, and push boundaries further. This creates competitive pressure to match their practices. Why handicap yourself when others don't? The pressure is real but shouldn't be decisive. Several considerations support maintaining ethical constraints even when competitors don't. Ethical violations carry risks that aren't immediately visible. Regulatory action, reputational damage, and customer backlash can turn short-term competitive gains into long-term losses. The competitor gaining advantage through questionable AI use may face consequences that you avoid by holding higher standards. What looks like competitive advantage today may become competitive liability tomorrow.

Trust is a durable advantage that unethical practices destroy. Customers who trust you resist competitive pressure. Relationships built on manipulation are fragile. When customers discover they've been manipulated, they leave and discourage others. Trust built through ethical practice survives competitive attacks that would destroy manipulated relationships. The competitor who won through manipulation has to keep manipulating. You don't. You have to live with yourself, and that matters more than it might seem. Professionals who compromise their values to match competitors often find the tradeoff wasn't worthwhile. Success achieved through practices you're not proud of doesn't feel like success. Integrity has personal value beyond strategic calculation. Your career will be long. Can you be proud of how you conducted it?

Industry norms shift based on what participants accept. If you lower standards to match competitors, you contribute to lowering industry norms. If you maintain standards despite pressure, you contribute to higher norms. Collective ethical improvement requires individual commitment even when it's costly. Someone has to hold the line for standards to exist at all. None of this makes competitive pressure disappear. Ethical constraints sometimes mean losing deals to competitors willing to do what you won't. The question is whether you're willing to accept that cost or whether winning by any means is your actual priority. The answer to that question defines what kind of professional you are.

Frameworks for Ethical Decision-Making

When guidelines are unclear, frameworks help structure ethical thinking. Several approaches prove useful for AI ethics in sales, and using multiple frameworks provides more complete ethical assessment than relying on any single test. The publicity test asks whether you'd be comfortable if your practice became public. If a journalist wrote a story about how your organization uses AI, would you be proud or embarrassed? Practices that require secrecy to be acceptable probably aren't acceptable. This test catches practices that seem fine in private but would look different under scrutiny. The role reversal test asks how you'd feel on the receiving end. If you were the customer and learned how your data was being used, how AI was targeting you, and what techniques were being applied to influence you, what would you think? Empathetic consideration of customer perspective often clarifies ethical assessment. It's easy to rationalize practices when you're the one benefiting from them.

The universalization test asks what would happen if everyone did this. If every company used AI in the way you're considering, would the overall result be acceptable? Some practices work only when others don't do them. Those practices usually fail the universalization test because they depend on being exceptional rather than universal. The stakeholder impact test considers effects on all affected parties, not just the company and immediate customer. Are there effects on third parties? On the broader market? On societal trust in AI? Narrow focus on direct parties misses important ethical dimensions. Your practices have ripple effects beyond the immediate transaction.

The long-term test considers consequences over extended time horizons. Practices that produce short-term gains but long-term harm look different when evaluated over appropriate timeframes. The salesperson focused on this quarter may make choices the salesperson thinking about their career would reject. Time horizon matters enormously for ethical assessment. These frameworks don't guarantee right answers. They structure thinking in ways that surface relevant considerations. When you're uncertain about a practice, run it through multiple frameworks. Consistent answers across frameworks suggest the assessment is sound. Conflicting answers suggest the situation deserves more careful thought.

The Strategic Case for Ethics

Ethics has strategic value beyond moral obligation. Ethical AI use produces better long-term business outcomes for several reasons that deserve explicit articulation, especially in organizations where moral arguments alone don't carry the day. Customer relationships deepen when built on ethical foundations. Customers who trust you become advocates. They provide referrals, resist competitive encroachment, and forgive occasional problems. These relationship benefits compound over time. Unethical practices produce transactions, not relationships. The deals close, but they don't lead anywhere. Ethical practice builds something durable. Talent retention improves in ethical organizations. Good salespeople want to work for ethical organizations. They don't want to manipulate customers or use practices they're ashamed of. Companies with strong ethical reputations attract and retain better talent than those known for pushing boundaries. Your ethics affect who wants to work with you.

Regulatory risk decreases for ethical organizations. AI regulation is expanding. Organizations that already operate ethically will find compliance easier than those that have to change problematic practices. Leading with ethics is cheaper than catching up to requirements. What's optional today may be mandatory tomorrow. Brand value grows through ethical reputation. Reputation for ethical practice contributes to brand strength. Companies known for respecting customers command premium positioning. The brand damage from ethical violations can exceed any gains the violations produced. Brand takes years to build and moments to destroy.

Sustainability increases with ethical practice. Unethical practices often work until they don't. A manipulated customer base churns. A data breach exposes negligent practices. A competitor calls out questionable tactics. A whistleblower goes public. Ethical practice is more sustainable because it doesn't depend on avoiding consequences. It can withstand scrutiny. The strategic case doesn't make ethics optional or purely instrumental. Ethics is required regardless of strategic benefit. But the strategic benefits provide additional reason for ethical practice and help make the case within organizations where moral arguments alone don't carry the day. Sometimes the right thing to do is also the smart thing to do.

Organizational Responsibility

Ethical AI use requires organizational commitment, not just individual good intentions. Organizations shape the context within which individuals make decisions. Without organizational support, even well-intentioned individuals will struggle to act ethically. Policies should be explicit. Organizations need clear statements about acceptable and unacceptable AI practices. Vague commitments to "ethical AI" don't guide behavior. Specific policies about data use, transparency, and manipulation provide actionable guidance. People need to know where the lines are.

Training should address ethics alongside technical operation. AI training that covers only how to use tools without addressing when not to use them is incomplete. Sales teams need education about ethical considerations specific to AI applications, not just technical operation. Capability without wisdom is dangerous. Incentives should align with ethical practice. If compensation rewards results without regard to methods, salespeople face pressure to compromise ethics for performance. Incentive structures should recognize ethical practice, not just outcomes. What you reward is what you get. Accountability should exist for ethical violations. Policies without enforcement are merely aspirational. When ethical violations occur, consequences should follow. Accountability demonstrates that ethical commitments are real. People notice whether standards are enforced.

Leadership should model ethics visibly. Executives and managers who push ethical boundaries signal that ethics is negotiable. Leaders who maintain ethical standards even when costly demonstrate genuine commitment. What leaders do matters more than what they say. Reporting channels should be safe for those who raise concerns. Salespeople who observe questionable practices need safe ways to raise concerns. Cultures that punish ethical questions suppress the feedback needed to maintain standards. If raising concerns is career-limiting, problems will go unreported. Organizations that leave ethics to individual conscience will have inconsistent ethical practice. Some individuals will make good choices. Others won't. Organizational commitment creates consistent standards that don't depend on individual variation.

Individual Responsibility

Organizational context matters, but individuals retain responsibility for their own choices. "I was following company policy" or "everyone else does it" don't eliminate individual ethical accountability. You are responsible for what you do, regardless of what others around you are doing. Know your own limits before pressure arrives. Consider what you won't do regardless of consequences. What practices would you refuse even if instructed? What lines won't you cross even if competitors do? Knowing your limits in advance makes holding them under pressure easier. The time to decide is before you face the choice.

Question instructions that seem wrong. Organizational authority doesn't override ethical judgment. If you're asked to do something that seems ethically problematic, raise the concern. You may be wrong, and the instruction may be appropriate. Or you may be right, and your question may prevent a mistake. Either way, you've exercised appropriate ethical agency. Silence isn't neutral. Accept responsibility for outcomes when your AI-assisted actions cause harm. Own that responsibility rather than deflecting to the technology or the organization. Taking responsibility is uncomfortable but maintains the integrity that matters for long-term professional standing. How you handle mistakes reveals character.

Develop ethical judgment through practice. Ethical reasoning improves with practice like any skill. Read about ethics. Discuss ethical questions with colleagues. Reflect on decisions after the fact. The investment in ethical capability pays off throughout your career. It's not a burden. It's a competency. Be willing to leave when necessary. Sometimes organizations don't change despite ethical concerns being raised. If you can't practice ethically within your organization and can't change the organization, leaving may be the right choice. Your career is long. Your integrity matters. Not every job is worth having. Some exits are victories.

Wesley worked for a company whose AI practices made him increasingly uncomfortable. Pressure to maximize data collection without clear customer consent, aggressive personalization that felt manipulative, and dismissal of his concerns by leadership created a situation where he couldn't work ethically within the organization's norms. He raised concerns through appropriate channels, documented his objections, and eventually left for a company whose practices aligned with his values. The departure cost him short-term income and disrupted his career trajectory. He doesn't regret it. He can explain his work proudly, and his new organization values the ethical perspective he brings. Some costs are worth paying.

The Path Forward

Ethics in AI-powered sales isn't a problem to solve once and forget. AI capabilities keep expanding. New ethical questions keep emerging. The ethical salesperson commits to ongoing engagement with these questions, not one-time compliance with a fixed ruleset. Ethics is a practice, not an achievement. This ongoing engagement connects to broader questions about where AI is heading and what it means for the sales profession. The ethical considerations raised here will become more pressing as AI capabilities grow. The practices established now will shape what becomes normal. The choices made by current professionals will influence the environment that future professionals inherit. What you do matters beyond your own career. The final chapter examines this trajectory. It considers what's coming, how to prepare for it, and what enduring principles will guide success regardless of how AI evolves. The road ahead is uncertain in its details but clear in its direction. Understanding that direction helps you navigate whatever specific developments emerge.

Chapter Fifteen

The Road Ahead

The Certainty of Change

Predicting the future is a fool's errand. The specific technologies, tools, and market conditions that will define sales five years from now can't be known with confidence. Anyone claiming certainty about details is selling something or fooling themselves. The history of technology prediction is littered with confident forecasts that turned out spectacularly wrong, and there's no reason to believe current predictions will prove more accurate.

But the direction of change is visible even when the destination isn't. AI capabilities will continue expanding. Automation will handle more tasks that currently require human attention. Human-machine collaboration will deepen in ways we're only beginning to understand. The integration patterns established today will evolve into patterns we can't yet imagine. This trajectory is clear even when its specific manifestations remain uncertain. The forces driving AI development show no signs of slowing, and the investment flowing into AI capabilities virtually guarantees continued advancement.

The goal of this chapter isn't prediction. It's preparation. Understanding the forces shaping the future helps you respond intelligently as that future arrives in whatever specific form it takes. Developing adaptive capacity matters more than guessing correctly about which specific technologies will prevail. The salespeople who succeed won't be those who predicted right. They'll be those who adapted well to whatever actually emerged. Prediction is a game you can't win. Adaptation is a capability you can build.

Capability Expansion

AI capabilities are expanding along multiple dimensions simultaneously, and this expansion shows no signs of slowing. Each advancement opens new possibilities for sales applications that weren't feasible before. Understanding these dimensions helps anticipate where AI assistance will grow most significant. Language capability continues improving at a remarkable pace. The systems that draft emails and summarize calls today will handle more complex communication tasks tomorrow. They'll write more persuasively, understand context more deeply, and generate content indistinguishable from human output. The gap between AI-generated and human-generated text will narrow until it's undetectable in most contexts. This isn't speculation about distant possibilities. It's extrapolation from capabilities that already exist and are improving rapidly. The email that clearly came from AI today will be indistinguishable from human writing tomorrow.

Reasoning capability is developing in ways that expand what AI can handle independently. Current AI systems recognize patterns and generate plausible outputs based on training data. Emerging systems demonstrate increasingly sophisticated reasoning: breaking down complex problems, considering multiple factors, weighing tradeoffs, and reaching conclusions through logical steps rather than pattern matching alone. This reasoning capability will enable AI to handle tasks that currently require human judgment, not because AI becomes human-like, but because many tasks that seem to require judgment actually require systematic analysis that AI can perform.

Multimodal capability extends AI beyond text into richer forms of understanding. Systems that process images, video, and audio alongside text can understand meetings by watching them, analyze products by looking at them, and assess sentiment from voice tone rather than just words. Sales applications will incorporate this multimodal understanding as it matures. The AI that only reads text today will see, hear, and integrate information across modalities tomorrow. This expansion creates possibilities for AI assistance that current text-based systems can't provide.

Action capability moves AI from analysis to execution in increasingly autonomous ways. Current systems recommend what to do. Emerging systems increasingly do it themselves: sending messages, updating records, scheduling meetings, and executing multi-step workflows without human intervention at each step. The boundary between AI as advisor and AI as actor is shifting steadily. This shift transforms AI from a tool you use into an agent that acts on your behalf.

Memory and context capabilities are expanding to create AI that behaves more like a knowledgeable colleague than a stateless tool. AI systems that remember past interactions, maintain awareness of ongoing situations, and connect information across time will provide fundamentally different assistance than systems that start fresh each interaction. A system that remembers your last hundred customer conversations and can reference them appropriately represents different capability than one that knows nothing about your history. This persistent awareness changes what AI can contribute to your work.

Each expansion increases what AI can handle in sales contexts. Tasks that require human attention today may not require it tomorrow. The expansion isn't linear. It accelerates as capabilities compound and reinforce each other. The pace of change over the next five years will almost certainly exceed the pace of the last five, which itself exceeded the pace before that. Preparing for this acceleration means building adaptive capacity rather than betting on specific predictions.

Autonomous Agents

The most significant near-term development is the emergence of AI agents that operate with increasing autonomy. Rather than waiting for human prompts and responding to specific requests, these agents pursue goals through self-directed action. This represents a fundamental shift in how AI contributes to sales work. Consider what an autonomous sales agent might do. Given a goal of generating qualified meetings, it could identify target accounts based on fit criteria, research relevant contacts within those accounts, craft personalized outreach tailored to each contact's situation, send messages at optimal times based on engagement patterns, respond to replies with appropriate follow-up, handle common objections without human involvement, schedule meetings when interest is established, and prepare briefings for the human salesperson who will conduct the meeting. Each step happens without human intervention. The agent reports results and escalates when situations exceed its capabilities or require human judgment.

This autonomy exists on a spectrum that's steadily expanding. Current AI tools typically wait for instructions and respond to specific prompts. Near-term developments enable AI to take initiative within bounded domains, acting toward goals with general guidance rather than step-by-step direction. Longer-term developments might produce agents that pursue complex goals across extended time horizons with minimal supervision, handling entire workflows that currently require continuous human attention.

The progression toward autonomy will be gradual and uneven rather than sudden and uniform. Some tasks will be delegated to autonomous agents earlier than others based on their complexity and stakes. High-stakes decisions will retain human oversight longer than routine actions. Situations requiring nuanced judgment will remain human responsibilities longer than situations with clear right answers. But the direction is unmistakable. AI will increasingly act rather than just advise, do rather than just recommend.

Sales professionals should prepare for this shift by thinking carefully about which activities they want to delegate and which they want to retain. Autonomous agents will handle whatever they're assigned. The judgment about what to assign remains human. Making that judgment well requires understanding what AI can handle reliably and what genuinely requires human attention. Delegating too little means missing efficiency gains that competitors capture. Delegating too much means losing capabilities that matter for customer relationships and strategic success. Finding the right balance becomes an essential skill.

The Augmentation Frontier

Even as AI takes over more tasks autonomously, augmentation of human capability remains central to how AI creates value in sales. The frontier of augmentation keeps advancing as AI capabilities grow, enabling humans to perform at levels they couldn't achieve alone. Real-time coaching moves beyond post-call analysis to in-the-moment guidance that shapes conversations as they happen. AI that listens to live conversations can suggest questions to ask, topics to address, and approaches to try while the conversation is unfolding. The salesperson wears an earpiece or watches a screen that provides continuous coaching adapted to what's happening in real time. This isn't reviewing calls after the fact to identify improvements. It's improving performance during the conversation itself, when it actually matters.

Predictive guidance anticipates what will happen next and helps salespeople navigate toward better outcomes. As you're speaking with a customer, AI predicts where the conversation is heading and suggests how to steer it more productively. It identifies buying signals you might miss because you're focused on what to say next. It warns of concerns developing beneath the surface before they become explicit objections. The guidance comes before problems manifest rather than after, enabling prevention rather than just response.

Emotional augmentation helps salespeople navigate emotional dynamics that significantly influence outcomes. AI that reads emotional state from voice tone, facial expression, word choice, and conversational patterns can advise on emotional approach: slow down because the customer seems overwhelmed, match their energy because they're excited, acknowledge frustration before pushing forward with your agenda. This augmentation supplements rather than replaces human emotional intelligence, adding analytical precision to intuitive reading of situations.

Knowledge augmentation provides instant access to relevant information during conversations when that information matters most. When a customer mentions a competitor, AI surfaces competitive intelligence you might not remember. When they ask about a feature, AI provides technical details beyond what you could recall. When they reference an industry development, AI offers context that enables more informed response. The salesperson becomes more knowledgeable in real time than any human could be from memory alone, turning conversations into opportunities to demonstrate expertise that builds credibility.

These augmentation capabilities transform what individual salespeople can accomplish in ways that compound over time. A person augmented with real-time AI assistance performs differently than a person relying solely on their own preparation and instincts. The augmented salesperson isn't replaced by AI. They're enhanced to a level of capability that unaugmented humans simply can't match. This creates competitive pressure to adopt augmentation and competitive advantage for those who use it effectively.

Changing Buyer Expectations

AI isn't just changing how salespeople work. It's changing how buyers behave and what they expect from sales interactions. These shifts in buyer expectations create pressure that accelerates AI adoption throughout the sales ecosystem. Buyers increasingly use AI themselves to prepare for purchasing decisions. They research options with AI assistance. They evaluate alternatives using AI analysis. They prepare for sales meetings with AI briefings that anticipate what salespeople will say. The information asymmetry that once favored sellers has flipped in many contexts. Buyers arrive informed, prepared, and sometimes skeptical of sales pitches that AI has helped them anticipate and critique. The buyer who knows nothing and relies on the salesperson to educate them is increasingly rare.

This informed buyer changes the sales dynamic fundamentally. Salespeople who rely on controlling information lose leverage because buyers can get that information elsewhere. Salespeople who provide value beyond available information become more important because they offer what self-service research can't provide. The bar for adding value rises because buyers can get basic information without talking to anyone. Generic pitches and standard presentations feel like a waste of time to buyers who've already done their homework.

Buyer expectations about responsiveness are shifting toward immediacy. When AI enables instant response, customers become impatient with delays. The two-day turnaround that once seemed reasonable feels slow when competitors respond in hours. Requests for information that require "getting back to you" feel like obstacles when others provide immediate answers. Speed expectations will continue accelerating as AI makes faster response possible and early adopters train buyers to expect it.

Personalization expectations are rising as well, shaped by AI experiences throughout buyers' lives. Buyers who experience AI-powered personalization in consumer contexts expect similar relevance in business contexts. Generic outreach that treats everyone the same feels increasingly inadequate and even disrespectful. The standard for what counts as personal attention keeps climbing. What impressed buyers last year feels generic this year. Organizations that can't deliver meaningful personalization will increasingly struggle to earn attention from buyers who expect better. These shifting expectations create pressure on sales organizations to adopt AI capabilities just to meet baseline buyer expectations. Falling behind on AI adoption means falling behind on meeting what buyers now consider normal. The gap between AI-enabled competitors and laggards will widen as expectations continue evolving. What's optional today becomes necessary tomorrow.

Role Evolution

Sales roles will continue evolving as AI capabilities expand and buyer expectations shift. Understanding potential trajectories helps with career preparation.

Transactional roles diminish. Sales jobs that primarily involve relaying information, processing orders, or executing scripted interactions face continued pressure. AI handles these functions more efficiently. Humans in these roles increasingly compete with automation that doesn't need benefits or sleep. The number of purely transactional sales positions will continue declining.

Consultative roles transform. Salespeople who provide advice, solve problems, and guide complex decisions remain important, but their work changes. AI handles research and analysis. Humans focus on judgment, relationship, and the creative aspects of problem-solving. The consultative salesperson of the future spends less time gathering information and more time applying wisdom to that information.

Orchestration roles emerge. As AI agents multiply, someone needs to direct them. New roles focus on designing AI workflows, setting objectives for autonomous agents, managing exceptions that agents can't handle, and ensuring that machine actions align with business strategy. These orchestration roles require understanding both sales and AI systems deeply.

Relationship roles elevate. The purely human aspects of sales relationships become more valuable as they become scarcer. Salespeople who excel at trust-building, emotional connection, and long-term relationship investment differentiate themselves from AI and from salespeople who rely too heavily on automation. Relationship expertise commands premium compensation.

Strategic roles expand. Strategy requires judgment that AI supports but doesn't replace. Which markets to pursue, how to position against competitors, when to walk away from deals, how to allocate resources across opportunities: these strategic decisions remain human. As AI handles execution, strategic contribution becomes the primary value that sales leaders provide.

Individual career paths will vary based on capabilities, preferences, and market opportunities. But understanding these general trajectories helps with planning development and positioning for emerging roles.

The Compression of Cycles

AI accelerates everything it touches, creating compression effects that reshape how sales works. One significant consequence is compression of sales cycles and competitive cycles that change market dynamics fundamentally. Sales cycles shorten as AI enables faster research, faster preparation, faster response, and faster execution. What once took weeks happens in days. What took days happens in hours. Decisions that required multiple meetings can be reached in one. Proposals that required days to prepare can be generated in hours. This compression benefits salespeople who can operate at speed and creates significant disadvantage for those who can't match the pace competitors set.

Competitive response accelerates in ways that change strategic dynamics. When competitors can analyze your moves and respond in days rather than months, competitive advantages become harder to sustain. The window for exploiting any innovation narrows before others catch up. Continuous adaptation replaces periodic strategy updates. The comfortable pace of annual planning cycles doesn't match the actual pace of competitive change. Learning cycles compress as well. AI enables faster experimentation and faster feedback on what works. Organizations that use this capability to learn rapidly gain compounding advantages over those that don't. The pace of improvement becomes itself a competitive differentiator. Organizations that learn slowly fall further behind with each passing month because faster learners keep pulling ahead.

Customer expectation cycles shorten as buyers adapt to new capabilities. Yesterday's innovation becomes today's baseline expectation. Buyers adapt to new capabilities quickly and begin expecting them from everyone. The refresh cycle on what counts as competitive capability accelerates. What impressed customers last quarter is standard this quarter and outdated next quarter. This compression creates pressure throughout the sales ecosystem that demands faster everything. Individuals must learn faster. Organizations must adapt faster. Strategies must evolve faster. The pace that felt demanding last year will feel leisurely next year. Success requires building capacity for continuous acceleration rather than hoping the pace will eventually stabilize.

New Forms of Competition

AI changes not just how competitors compete but who the competitors are. The competitive landscape is shifting in ways that create new threats and new opportunities. AI-native companies build sales capability around AI from the start rather than retrofitting AI into processes designed for human execution. They don't try to bolt AI onto legacy processes. They design processes assuming AI handles what AI does best. These native competitors operate with structural advantages in efficiency and capability that retrofitted competitors struggle to match because their processes weren't built to leverage AI fully.

Platform competition intensifies as AI vendors integrate more deeply into sales workflows. The company that provides your AI sales platform accumulates data that improves their AI, which attracts more customers, which provides more data. This dynamic produces winner-take-most outcomes in some market segments. Platform choices become strategic decisions with long-term implications beyond the immediate functionality purchased.

Direct-to-customer competition increases as AI enables smaller organizations to reach buyers that once required large sales forces to access. A startup with AI-powered outreach can contact more prospects than a mid-sized company with traditional sales. Distribution advantages that protected established players erode as AI democratizes reach. Scale matters less when AI provides leverage that was previously only available through headcount.

Automated competition emerges from AI agents that compete directly with human salespeople for buyer attention and business. In some contexts, buyers prefer interacting with AI: it's faster, available constantly, doesn't pressure them, and provides immediate answers. Salespeople compete not just with other salespeople but with the option of no salesperson at all. This competition forces focus on contexts where human involvement creates clear value that AI alternatives can't match.

These competitive dynamics require strategic response that accounts for where competitive advantage actually lies. Competing against AI-native companies means finding advantages they can't easily replicate, typically in relationship depth and human judgment. Navigating platform competition means making wise choices about which platforms to build on. Responding to automated competition means focusing on contexts where human involvement creates clear buyer value that justifies the friction of human interaction.

Preparing Without Predicting

Specific predictions about future technologies will be wrong. Anyone who tells you exactly what the technology landscape will look like in

THE ROAD AHEAD 221

five years is guessing, regardless of how confident they sound. The useful preparation isn't predicting correctly but building adaptive capacity that responds effectively to whatever emerges.

Build foundational capability that transcends any particular technology or tool. Deep sales competence transfers across technology changes because the fundamentals don't change even when the tools do. The salesperson who truly understands buyer psychology, value communication, and relationship building remains effective regardless of which specific tools prevail. Foundational capability provides stable ground from which to adapt to whatever changes arrive.

Develop learning agility as a core competency. The ability to learn new tools and approaches quickly matters more than expertise in any particular tool that might be displaced. Practice learning itself. Build habits of experimentation that make encountering new tools comfortable rather than threatening. Develop comfort with not knowing everything and figuring it out as you go. Learning agility is itself a trainable skill that improves with deliberate practice.

Maintain technology engagement even when specific technologies aren't immediately relevant to your current work. Stay current with AI developments through reading, experimentation, and conversation. Try new tools when they emerge. Maintain awareness of what's becoming possible. This engagement ensures you see developments as they become relevant rather than after competitors have already responded and captured the advantages of early adoption.

Cultivate human skills that AI can't replicate. The capabilities that AI can't match become more valuable as AI handles more of what it can do. Invest in trust-building, emotional intelligence, creative problem-solving, and ethical judgment. These human skills differentiate you from automation and from competitors who neglect them while focusing only on AI proficiency.

Build resilient networks of relationships with other sales professionals, technology experts, and industry contacts. These networks provide information and opportunity that solitary preparation can't match. Networks share insights about what's working and what's emerging. They provide early warning of changes and access to opportunities. Investing in relationships pays compound returns over time.

Preserve financial flexibility that provides options when changes require response. Career transitions are easier to navigate with resources that enable pivots if needed. Maintain savings that enable taking risks or absorbing disruptions. Avoid financial commitments that lock you into situations that may become untenable. Flexibility enables adaptation that rigidity prevents. This preparation doesn't guarantee success. Nothing does in an uncertain world. But it positions you to respond effectively to changes that can't be specifically anticipated. Adaptation, not prediction, is the winning strategy when the future can't be known.

The Enduring Human Element

Through all the technological change, certain human elements remain central to sales success. These elements won't be displaced regardless of how AI evolves because they reflect needs that technology doesn't address.

Purpose endures. Sales exists to help customers solve problems and achieve goals. This purpose precedes any particular technology and will outlast current technologies. The salesperson who genuinely cares about customer outcomes provides value that transcends tools because that genuine care creates something customers can't get from automation.

Trust endures. Complex purchases require trust that only humans can establish. Customers buy important solutions from people they trust to deliver what's promised, to tell the truth even when it's uncomfortable, and to stand behind commitments when things go wrong. No AI advancement changes the human need for trusted relationships in high-stakes decisions where a lot rides on the outcome.

Judgment endures. Deciding what's right, what's appropriate, and what serves long-term interests requires wisdom that AI can inform but not replace. The hard calls that define sales careers remain human responsibilities because they involve values and priorities that only humans can weigh.

Connection endures. People want to do business with other people. They want to be understood as individuals, not processed as data. They want relationships that acknowledge their humanity. This need for human connection persists regardless of what AI can do because it reflects something fundamental about human nature.

These enduring elements provide compass heading through technological change. When disoriented by the pace of AI development, return to these fundamentals. What serves the customer? What builds trust? What reflects good judgment? What creates genuine connection? These questions guide effective action in any environment because they address needs that don't change.

Embracing the Journey

The future of sales and AI isn't a destination to reach. It's a journey to navigate. The technologies will keep evolving. The competitive dynamics will keep shifting. The buyer expectations will keep rising. There is no stable state where you can stop adapting and coast on what you've already learned. This reality might seem exhausting. Constant change does demand continuous response. But it also offers continuous opportunity. Every shift creates new ways to succeed. Every emerging capability offers new tools for those who learn to use them. The professionals who embrace continuous adaptation find more opportunity than those who seek stability that doesn't exist. The change that threatens those who resist it rewards those who engage with it.

The embrace involves orientation rather than specific actions. It means approaching change with curiosity rather than fear. It means viewing new capabilities as possibilities rather than threats. It means accepting uncertainty as permanent rather than waiting for certainty that won't arrive. It means finding satisfaction in growth rather than comfort in stasis.

Greta has worked in sales for over two decades. She's seen technologies come and go, strategies rise and fall, and market conditions shift repeatedly. The common thread through her successful career isn't any particular skill or tool. It's her orientation toward change itself. She treats every development as interesting rather than threatening. She experiments constantly with new approaches. She maintains relationships with people at many career stages who expose her to different perspectives. She's never bored because she's always learning. The current AI shift doesn't frighten her. It energizes her. She sees opportunity where others see threat. This orientation, more than any specific capability, explains her sustained success across decades of change.

The Integration Imperative

Throughout this book, one theme has recurred: the integration of AI capability with human excellence produces results neither achieves alone. This integration isn't optional. It's imperative for success in modern sales. Those who master integration will outperform those who rely on either capability alone. AI without human judgment is dangerous. It makes mistakes that humans would catch. It optimizes for measurable outcomes while missing unmeasurable value. It processes without understanding context. It acts without wisdom about consequences. AI systems lack the values, relationships, and contextual awareness that humans bring. Relying on AI alone produces efficiency without effectiveness, speed without wisdom.

Human effort without AI assistance is inefficient. It limits reach that AI could extend. It consumes time on tasks AI could handle. It misses patterns AI could detect. It operates with less information than AI could provide. Humans working without AI assistance compete at a disadvantage against those who leverage AI's capabilities. The integration requires both capabilities present and properly combined. AI handles information processing, pattern recognition, routine execution, and scale. Humans handle relationship building, judgment application, creative problem-solving, and ethical navigation. Each contributes what it does well. Neither tries to do what the other does better. The division of labor reflects actual strengths rather than habit or fear.

This integration is a skill that must be developed. It doesn't happen automatically when AI tools are available. Salespeople must learn how to leverage AI effectively, when to trust AI and when to override it, and how to combine AI assistance with their own capability. The learning takes time and practice. But the capability that results is the defining competency of successful modern sales professionals.

Closing Thoughts

This book has explored how AI and sales work together. We examined what AI can do: finding prospects, understanding customers, personalizing at scale, supporting negotiations, and creating efficiency. We examined what AI can't do: building trust, reading nuanced situations, exercising judgment, and bringing genuine human presence to relationships. We explored how to lead AI-augmented teams, build technology stacks, measure impact, and navigate ethical challenges.

The synthesis across these chapters is straightforward. AI and sales aren't competing forces. They're complementary capabilities. AI handles information, pattern recognition, and routine tasks better than humans. Humans handle trust, relationship, judgment, and creative problem-solving better than AI. The combination produces results neither achieves alone.

The practical implication is equally straightforward. Develop both sets of capability. Build AI competence so you can leverage what AI offers. Build human skills so you can contribute what AI can't. The salespeople who combine both will outperform those who have only one. The orientation this requires isn't complicated either. Stay curious about emerging AI capabilities. Stay grounded in timeless sales fundamentals. Stay focused on serving customers genuinely. Stay committed to continuous development. Stay open to change that can't be predicted.

Sales is a human profession that AI is transforming. It will remain a human profession after that transformation. The humans involved will work differently than they did before. They'll accomplish more with AI assistance than they could without it. They'll focus on different activities as AI handles more of what used to require human attention. But they'll still be essential to the complex work of helping customers solve problems and achieve goals. Your role in this evolving profession depends on choices you make. You can resist AI and watch capability accumulate in competitors' hands. You can embrace AI uncritically and lose the human skills that differentiate. Or you can thoughtfully integrate AI capability with human excellence, building a practice that combines the best of both.

The choice is yours. The future is being written now by the actions of people like you who are figuring out how to navigate this moment. The decisions you make about learning, development, and adaptation shape not just your own career but the profession that emerges from this transition. Make those decisions wisely. The opportunity is substantial. The path is clear enough to begin even if the destination remains uncertain. The journey starts with the next choice you make about how to develop, how to work, and how to serve your customers in a world where AI and human capability increasingly combine. The future of sales belongs to those who build it. Build something good.

Chapter Sixteen

Self-Assessment Guide: Your AI-Augmented Sales Readiness

Introduction

Reading about AI and sales is valuable. Applying what you've learned is essential. This self-assessment helps you evaluate your current capabilities, identify gaps, and prioritize development. The goal isn't achieving perfect scores. It's gaining honest awareness of where you stand and where to focus your efforts. Complete this assessment thoughtfully rather than quickly. Consider specific examples from your recent work rather than answering based on general impressions. Return to this assessment periodically to track your progress and identify new development priorities as AI capabilities and your own skills evolve.

Part One: AI Foundations and Adoption

This section evaluates your fundamental understanding of AI and your current adoption of AI tools in your sales work.

Understanding AI Capabilities

Consider how well you understand what AI can and cannot do in sales contexts. Rate yourself on a scale of 1-5, where 1 means "not at all" and 5 means "completely":

- I can explain to a colleague how AI tools I use actually work, not just what buttons to push but what's happening underneath. ___

- I understand the difference between AI that recognizes patterns and AI that reasons through problems, and I know which type I'm using in different tools. ___

- I can identify situations where AI recommendations are likely to be reliable versus situations where I should be skeptical. ___

- I understand what data my AI tools need to function effectively and how data quality affects their performance. ___

- I can articulate what AI fundamentally cannot do in sales, regardless of how advanced the technology becomes. ___

Add your scores for this section: ___ / 25

Current Tool Adoption

Consider your actual use of AI tools in daily sales work. Be honest about consistent use rather than occasional experimentation. Rate yourself on a scale of 1-5, where 1 means "never" and 5 means "consistently integrated into my workflow":

- I use AI assistance for prospect research and account intelligence. ___

- I use AI tools to help draft and personalize customer communications. ___

- I use conversation intelligence to analyze my calls and identify improvement opportunities. ___

- I use AI-powered tools for meeting preparation and follow-up summarization. ___

- I use AI assistance for proposal and document generation. ___

- I use AI tools for scheduling and administrative task automation. ___

- I actively experiment with new AI capabilities as they become available. ___

Add your scores for this section: ___ / 35

Interpreting Your AI Foundations Score

If your combined score for Part One is 45-60, you have strong AI foundations. Focus on optimization and staying current with emerging capabilities.

If your score is 30-44, you have moderate foundations with clear room for growth. Identify specific tools you're underutilizing and commit to deeper adoption.

If your score is below 30, AI adoption should be an immediate priority. Start with one or two high-impact tools and build proficiency before expanding.

Part Two: AI-Assisted Sales Activities

This section evaluates how effectively you leverage AI across the core sales activities covered in this book.

Prospecting and Lead Development

Think about your actual prospecting practices over the past quarter. Rate yourself on a scale of 1-5, where 1 means "strongly disagree" and 5 means "strongly agree":

- I use AI-powered tools to identify prospects who match my ideal customer profile rather than relying solely on purchased lists or manual research. ___

- I leverage intent data and behavioral signals to prioritize prospects showing buying readiness. ___

- I use AI to research prospects thoroughly before outreach, going beyond basic company information to understand their specific situation. ___

- My prospecting approach produces higher-quality opportunities than it did before I adopted AI assistance. ___

- I regularly review and refine my AI-assisted prospecting process based on what's actually working. ___

Add your scores for this section: ___ / 25

Customer Understanding

Consider how well you use AI to develop deep understanding of your customers and prospects. Rate yourself on a scale of 1-5:

- I use AI tools to aggregate and synthesize information about customers from multiple sources into actionable intelligence. ___

- I leverage conversation intelligence to identify patterns in what customers say, how they say it, and what topics generate engagement or resistance. ___

- I use AI to track changes in customer behavior, sentiment, and engagement that might signal shifting needs or concerns. ___

- I use predictive insights to anticipate customer needs before they express them explicitly. ___

- I maintain comprehensive, AI-assisted records that allow me to reference past interactions accurately and build on previous conversations. ___

Add your scores for this section: ___ / 25

Personalization at Scale

Evaluate how effectively you deliver personalized engagement to your customers and prospects. Rate yourself on a scale of 1-5:

- I use AI to customize communications based on individual recipient characteristics rather than sending generic messages. ___

- My AI-assisted personalization goes beyond surface-level customization like inserting names and company references to address recipients' actual situations and concerns. ___

- I review and refine AI-generated content to add human insight and ensure authentic voice before sending. ___

- I use AI to optimize timing and channel selection for outreach based on individual recipient patterns. ___

- My personalized outreach produces measurably better response rates than generic approaches. ___

Add your scores for this section: ___ / 25

Efficiency and Productivity

Consider how effectively you use AI to recover time and increase productivity. Rate yourself on a scale of 1-5:

- AI automation has significantly reduced the time I spend on administrative tasks like CRM updates, scheduling, and data entry. ___

- I use AI to prepare for meetings more thoroughly in less time than manual preparation would require. ___

- I have deliberately reinvested time saved by AI into higher-value activities like customer engagement and relationship building. ___

- I can quantify approximately how much time AI saves me weekly and how that time gets used. ___

- My overall productivity, measured by outcomes rather than just activity, has improved since adopting AI tools. ___

Add your scores for this section: ___ / 25

Interpreting Your AI-Assisted Activities Score

If your combined score for Part Two is 80-100, you're leveraging AI effectively across core sales activities. Focus on continuous refinement and staying ahead of evolving capabilities.

If your score is 50-79, you have solid practices in some areas but gaps in others. Identify your lowest-scoring section and prioritize improvement there.

If your score is below 50, significant opportunity exists to improve your AI-assisted sales practices. Focus on building proficiency in one area at a time rather than trying to improve everything simultaneously.

Part Three: Human Skills That AI Can't Replace

This section evaluates the distinctly human capabilities that become more valuable as AI handles more routine tasks.

Trust and Relationship Building

Consider your effectiveness at building trust and maintaining meaningful customer relationships. Rate yourself on a scale of 1-5, where 1 means "significant development needed" and 5 means "consistent strength":

- Customers tell me things they don't tell other vendors, indicating they trust me with sensitive information. ___

- I maintain relationships with customers that survive problems, competitive pressure, and personnel changes. ___

- I invest in understanding customers as people, not just as accounts, and they recognize that genuine interest. ___

- I follow through reliably on commitments, even small ones, building trust through consistent dependability. ___

- Former customers maintain contact with me and refer others to me based on relationship quality rather than just transaction outcomes. ___

Add your scores for this section: ___ / 25

Judgment and Strategic Thinking

Evaluate your ability to exercise judgment in complex situations where data alone doesn't provide answers. Rate yourself on a scale of 1-5:

- I make sound decisions about which opportunities to pursue and which to decline based on strategic fit rather than just pursuing everything. ___

- I recognize when AI recommendations don't fit a specific situation and know when to override them based on factors the AI can't see. ___

- I effectively navigate complex political dynamics within customer organizations, understanding who influences decisions and how to work with multiple stakeholders. ___

- I can identify when a deal isn't right for the customer and have the integrity to say so, even when it costs me a sale. ___

- I think strategically about my territory, accounts, and career rather than just reacting to immediate opportunities and demands. ___

Add your scores for this section: ___ / 25

Emotional Intelligence and Adaptability

Consider your ability to read situations, adapt to different people, and navigate emotional dynamics. Rate yourself on a scale of 1-5:

- I accurately read non-verbal cues and emotional undertones in customer interactions and adjust my approach accordingly. ___

- I adapt my communication style effectively for different personalities, roles, and cultural contexts. ___

- I remain effective under pressure, maintaining composure and clear thinking when stakes are high or situations become tense. ___

- I handle objections and difficult conversations constructively, addressing concerns without becoming defensive or dismissive. ___

- I recover well from setbacks, using failures as learning opportunities rather than dwelling on disappointment. ___

Add your scores for this section: ___ / 25

Creative Problem-Solving

Evaluate your ability to find innovative solutions when standard approaches don't work. Rate yourself on a scale of 1-5:

- I find creative ways to structure deals that address customer constraints while meeting business requirements. ___

- I identify solutions to customer problems that go beyond standard offerings, sometimes involving resources or approaches others wouldn't consider. ___

- When negotiations reach impasse, I can reframe discussions in ways that create new possibilities for agreement. ___

- I bring fresh perspectives to customer challenges rather than simply presenting standard solutions. ___

- Customers come to me with problems because they expect I'll help them think through issues, not just sell them products. ___

Add your scores for this section: ___ / 25

Interpreting Your Human Skills Score

If your combined score for Part Three is 80-100, your human capabilities are strong. Continue developing these skills while ensuring AI proficiency keeps pace.

If your score is 50-79, you have solid human skills with room for growth. Consider which areas most directly affect your success and prioritize development there.

If your score is below 50, investing in human skill development should be a priority alongside AI adoption. These capabilities become more valuable, not less, as AI handles more routine tasks.

Part Four: Ethical Awareness and Practice

This section evaluates your awareness of ethical considerations in AI-powered sales and your commitment to ethical practice.

Ethical Awareness

Consider how thoroughly you've thought through the ethical dimensions of AI use in your sales work. Rate yourself on a scale of 1-5, where 1 means "haven't considered" and 5 means "thoroughly considered and have clear positions":

- I have thought carefully about what customer data I'm comfortable gathering and using, and what crosses ethical lines regardless of what's technically possible. ___

- I understand the difference between personalization that serves customers and manipulation that exploits them, and I know where my own boundaries are. ___

- I have considered when AI involvement in customer interactions should be disclosed and when non-disclosure becomes problematic. ___

- I have thought about fairness implications of AI tools I use, including whether they might disadvantage certain customer groups in ways I wouldn't endorse. ___

- I have clear personal limits on practices I won't engage in regardless of competitive pressure or organizational expectations. ___

Add your scores for this section: ___ / 25

Ethical Practice

Consider whether your actual behavior reflects your ethical awareness. Rate yourself on a scale of 1-5, where 1 means "rarely" and 5 means "consistently":

- I review AI-generated content to ensure it doesn't misrepresent or manipulate, rather than sending whatever the system produces. ___

- I'm transparent with customers about AI involvement when they would reasonably want to know. ___

- I decline to use AI capabilities in ways that would make me uncomfortable if customers knew exactly what I was doing. ___

- I would raise concerns if asked to use AI in ways I considered unethical, even if it created professional difficulty. ___

- I consider the long-term customer relationship, not just the immediate transaction, when deciding how to use AI tools. ___

Add your scores for this section: ___ / 25

Interpreting Your Ethics Score

If your combined score for Part Four is 40-50, you have strong ethical awareness and practice. Continue developing your ethical thinking as AI capabilities expand.

If your score is 25-39, you have moderate ethical awareness with room for deeper consideration. Revisit Chapter 14 and think through the frameworks presented there.

If your score is below 25, ethical development should be a priority. AI power without ethical grounding creates risk for you, your customers, and your organization.

Part Five: Career Readiness and Adaptability

This section evaluates your preparation for continued evolution of AI in sales.

Learning Orientation

Consider how you approach ongoing development in a rapidly changing environment. Rate yourself on a scale of 1-5, where 1 means "strongly disagree" and 5 means "strongly agree":

- I regularly dedicate time to learning about AI developments relevant to sales, even when not required by my organization. ___

- I experiment with new AI tools and capabilities rather than waiting until adoption becomes mandatory. ___

- I seek feedback on my performance and use it constructively rather than defensively. ___

- I learn from both my successes and failures, taking time to understand what worked and what didn't. ___

- I actively seek out people who know things I don't and learn from their perspectives and experiences. ___

Add your scores for this section: ___ / 25

Adaptability and Resilience

Evaluate your capacity to adapt to change and maintain effectiveness through disruption. Rate yourself on a scale of 1-5:

- I approach new technologies and methods with curiosity rather than resistance or anxiety. ___

- I can adjust my approach when something isn't working rather than persisting with familiar methods that no longer produce results. ___

- I maintain effectiveness during periods of significant change rather than becoming paralyzed by uncertainty. ___

- I have navigated previous technology transitions successfully and applied lessons from those experiences to current changes. ___

- I have contingency plans and resources that would allow me to navigate career disruption if my current role changed significantly. ___

Add your scores for this section: ___ / 25

Professional Network and Visibility

Consider the strength of your professional network and positioning for future opportunities. Rate yourself on a scale of 1-5:

- I maintain active relationships with other sales professionals who share insights about what's working in AI adoption. ___

- I have connections with people outside my current organization who could provide opportunities or information if needed. ___

- I'm known within my professional community for competence in areas that will remain valuable as AI evolves. ___

- I contribute to others' development, not just my own, building relationships through mutual support. ___

- I could find a new position relatively quickly if needed because of my reputation and relationships. ___

Add your scores for this section: ___ / 25

Interpreting Your Career Readiness Score

If your combined score for Part Five is 60-75, you're well-positioned for continued evolution. Maintain your learning orientation and network investment.

If your score is 40-59, you have moderate career readiness with clear opportunities for improvement. Identify whether learning, adaptability, or network needs most attention.

If your score is below 40, career resilience should be a priority. The pace of change in AI-augmented sales rewards those who invest in adaptability.

Part Six: For Sales Leaders

Complete this section only if you have responsibility for leading others. This evaluates your effectiveness at building AI capability across your team or organization.

Building Team AI Capability

Consider how effectively you develop AI competence in the people you lead. Rate yourself on a scale of 1-5, where 1 means "not at all" and 5 means "very effectively":

- I have established clear expectations that AI tool adoption is standard practice, not optional, for my team. ___
- I provide adequate training and support for AI tools, going beyond basic tool operation to effective integration into workflows. ___
- I include AI proficiency in hiring criteria and evaluate candidates for learning agility and technology comfort. ___
- I coach team members on effective AI use, not just outcomes,

helping them improve how they leverage AI assistance. ___

- I model effective AI use myself rather than asking others to do things I don't do. ___

Add your scores for this section: ___ / 25

Creating Conditions for Success

Evaluate how well you create the organizational conditions that enable AI-augmented sales success. Rate yourself on a scale of 1-5:

- My team has access to AI tools that genuinely help their work, selected based on actual needs rather than vendor relationships or trends. ___

- Our data infrastructure enables AI tools to function effectively, with clean, comprehensive data flowing where it needs to go. ___

- Performance expectations and compensation structures account for AI capabilities, expecting more from AI-augmented salespeople while rewarding effective AI use. ___

- I protect human elements of sales culture, including customer connection and team collaboration, even as automation expands. ___

- I make technology decisions thoughtfully, evaluating tools systematically rather than reacting to pitches or competitive pressure. ___

Add your scores for this section: ___ / 25

Managing Change

Consider how effectively you lead your team through ongoing AI-related change. Rate yourself on a scale of 1-5:

- I communicate clearly about why AI changes are happening and how they benefit the team, not just the organization. ___

- I involve team members in AI-related decisions where appropriate, building commitment through participation. ___

- I address resistance constructively, distinguishing legitimate concerns from general discomfort and responding appropriately to each. ___

- I support the team through adoption challenges, maintaining patience and providing resources during learning curves. ___

- I celebrate AI-enabled wins and share success stories that build momentum for continued adoption. ___

Add your scores for this section: ___ / 25

Interpreting Your Leadership Score

If your combined score for Part Six is 60-75, you're effectively building AI capability across your team. Continue developing your leadership approach as AI capabilities evolve.

If your score is 40-59, you're providing moderate leadership with clear opportunities for improvement. Identify your lowest-scoring area and prioritize development there.

If your score is below 40, leadership development in AI contexts should be a priority. Your team's AI success depends significantly on the conditions and support you provide.

Calculating Your Overall Profile

Transfer your section scores here:

Part One: AI Foundations and Adoption ___ / 60

Part Two: AI-Assisted Sales Activities ___ / 100

Part Three: Human Skills ___ / 100

Part Four: Ethical Awareness and Practice ___ / 50

Part Five: Career Readiness and Adaptability ___ / 75

Part Six: Sales Leadership (if applicable) ___ / 75

Identifying Development Priorities

Rather than focusing on your total score, examine the pattern across sections. The most valuable insight comes from identifying relative strengths and weaknesses. Your strongest sections indicate capabilities you can leverage and potentially help others develop. Consider how you might contribute to colleagues or team members who are weaker in your areas of strength.

Your weakest sections indicate priority development areas. Focus improvement efforts on your one or two lowest-scoring sections rather than trying to improve everything simultaneously. Concentrated effort produces faster progress than diffuse attention. Sections where you scored moderately represent maintenance areas. Continue developing these capabilities but prioritize areas of clear weakness first.

Creating Your Development Plan

Based on your assessment, identify:

- Your top development priority (lowest-scoring section):
  _____

- Specific actions you will take in the next 30 days:
  _____

- How you will measure progress:
  _____

- When you will reassess (90 days is recommended):
  _____

Reassessment Guidance

Return to this assessment quarterly to track progress and identify new priorities. As you develop in weak areas, other areas may emerge as new priorities. As AI capabilities evolve, questions that seemed irrelevant may become important. Treat this assessment as a living tool rather than a one-time exercise. The goal isn't achieving perfect scores across all sections. It's maintaining awareness of your capabilities and continuously developing in ways that position you for success as AI and sales continue evolving together.

Final Reflection

This assessment measures where you are, not where you'll stay. Every capability evaluated here can be developed. Every weakness identified can become a strength with focused effort over time. The salespeople who thrive in AI-augmented environments aren't those who started with the most capability. They're those who committed to continuous development and followed through on that commitment. Your current scores matter less than what you do next. The integration of AI capability with human excellence that this book describes isn't an end state to achieve. It's an ongoing practice to pursue. Each day offers opportunities to leverage AI more effectively, develop human skills more deeply, and serve customers more genuinely. Use this assessment to guide that ongoing development. Return to it regularly to track progress and refine priorities. Share it with colleagues who might benefit from similar reflection. The journey of becoming an excellent AI-augmented sales professional continues as long as you're willing to keep learning and growing. The future belongs to those who build it. Start building.

www.ingramcontent.com/pod-product-compliance
Lightning Source LLC
LaVergne TN
LVHW021336080526
838202LV00004B/199